To Horthingnao Raikhan

*This book was born as a **birthday gift**, written by a brother for his sister. But the pages found a life of their own. It was never meant to travel this far yet love always finds a way.*

A

LOVE LETTER

TO MY

SISTER

Author: Jimson Rk

ISBN: 978-93-340-7748-3

Author Information:

Email = Jimsonrk@gmail.com
Social media account
Linkedin @Jimson Rk
Personal Instagram @ Jimson Rk
Quora @Jimson Rk

*Product available on digital only/-

Cover and interior design by the author

I can make a good cup of coffee.

SPOTLIGHT

Language style:

Growing up in India, where languages mix as easily as people do, I came to see how powerful words can be. They shape the way we understand each other, how we connect, and sometimes, how we stay apart. For many of us, English is a second language. It opens doors, "yes" but it can also feel heavy, especially when it's wrapped in complex phrases or dense writing. I've often seen beautiful ideas get lost behind complicated language, turning something meaningful into something hard to reach. So instead of grand words, I am choosing a different path for this book, one where the message matters more than the packaging. I've chosen to keep the words simple so the ideas can reach you without barriers

I chose to step away from the usual approach of impressing readers with grand vocabulary. Instead, I've embraced a casual, conversational tone like we're sharing a cup of coffee, or better yet, a steaming cup of *Garam Chai*, while chatting about ideas that matter. I want you to feel at ease, as though you're hearing from a friend, not sitting through a lecture. No pretentiousness, just the warmth of familiarity.

At its core, my writing is about building connection, not creating distance. You'll find language here that's simple, open, and unguarded. I've let go of literary jargon so the ideas can breathe and meet you where you are. My thoughts are meant to flow naturally, without asking you to pause and decode them. Let's just say I care more about you understanding my message than showcasing my vocabulary. Or, to put it another way, I'd rather connect with you than impress a dictionary.

Introduction

From a Brother's to His Sister and the World

For over twenty-eight years, I have wandered through the changing light of day and the hush of night. I have stumbled more times than I can count, and each misstep has taught me something about life, love, and what it means to be human. I haven't mastered it all, not even close, but I have gathered a few truths along the way. And now, I feel a subtle ache to pass them on to my sister still in her early twenties, just beginning to shape her place in the world.

These words are for her, but also for you if you've ever paused and wondered how to live fully without losing yourself in the noise, how to love the world without being broken by it.

This book grew from a single question: **How can we live meaningfully without becoming strangers to our own souls?** It is a journey into that question, a path lit by shared reflections, silent revelations, and hard-won peace. It invites you to build a better relationship with yourself, to understand others with compassion, and to stop treating life as something you must survive, rather than something you are meant to grow within.

At its heart, this book is built on letters, personal, handwritten thoughts penned like old love notes to life itself. I believe, in a world of voice notes, fleeting texts, and endless scrolling, letter-writing offers something rare: stillness, presence, intimacy. Unlike a hurried conversation or a distracted message, a letter waits for you. It gives you space. It listens back.

I wrote these letters to my sisters as a way of reaching them in moments when words might falter, when our moods might not align, or when life pulls us too far from one another. Over time, I realized that these reflections weren't only for them, they belonged to anyone walking through uncertainty, seeking clarity, or longing for a deeper sense of purpose.

These pages carry fragments of my journey, not as answers, but as small lanterns lit by the moments I've lived and the lessons I'm still learning. I don't hold them high as if to guide the way, but offer them beside you, in case their light might ease your next step. Like a traveler scribbling thoughts in the margins of a worn journal, I share these reflections in the hope that something within them stirs a gentle recognition in you, of your own strength, your own truth, and the tender courage it takes to live with intention.

I don't write to instruct. I write to remind you of what you already know deep within that you are not here to drift through life, numbed by habit or hardened by disappointment. You are here to feel, to love, and to live fully.

This book is for anyone who has ever wanted to understand their own mind better, to soften where life has made them rigid, and to rise, yes, rise, into a more honest, meaningful version of themselves. It is a call to pause, reflect, and walk through this world with both wonder and intention.

It opens a window into my own questions, my stumbles, and the insights that followed. What I've gathered here was shaped not by certainty, but by curiosity and a care longing to understand this life and to offer something that is true in return.

And after all, who among us doesn't long to peek into a personal diary, to read something raw and real, something that doesn't try to sell a perfect life but speaks instead to the sacred mess of becoming?

May these pages offer you something steady in the shifting winds. May they remind you of your worth. And may they guide you kindly and powerfully.

Become the Story You Want to Tell

This life holds meaning not in promises but in presence, waiting to be lived. A sense of direction doesn't come from what the world tells you, but from what you slowly begin to understand about yourself.

Life's journey has no fixed map. It bends and shifts, bringing both opportunities and challenges that shape who we are. Along the way, we're given one powerful gift: the ability to **choose**. In each moment, we decide between fear and courage, illusion and honesty, momentary relief and lasting peace.

Each decision you take shapes the story you're writing, whether you notice it or not. Every choice becomes a sentence in the book of your becoming.

You are the hero of your story, the main character in every scene. The choices you make and the way you respond are your lines. The mindset you carry, the way you treat others and the values you hold becomes the themes that repeat throughout your life's story.

Every decision you make today shapes the life you'll step into tomorrow. That's the essence of **karma**—not a mystical idea, but a simple truth: *actions create consequences.* When we act out of impulse, ego, or pressure, we often trade long-term peace for short-term comfort.

Wisdom sometimes means knowing what to wait for. Like choosing ten apples in the evening rather than one in the morning and going hungry the rest of the day. It's not about ignoring the present, it's about understanding what matters most in the long run. Fulfilment doesn't come from chasing everything at once; it comes when your thoughts, words, and actions begin to reflect your deeper values. When your daily life aligns with the person you hope to become.

You don't need to shrink your dreams to fit your current circumstances or silence your truth to please others. Dare to imagine a future larger than where you stand now, and take small, honest steps toward it.

Forget what others think for a moment and ask yourself:
What kind of life feels true to me?
What do I want to leave behind, not in things, but in meaning?

Most people never pause long enough to ask themselves those questions. They move through years on autopilot, chasing approval, mistaking movement for progress. But the reality is what we choose, or fail to choose, eventually shapes the texture of our days.

I've seen so many bright, capable people stay stuck, doing work that drains them, all because they chose what felt safe and socially accepted. And I've also seen people who took a different path. They listened to their inner self and acted with the command that comes from within, not from outside world.

In the process, there will be rejection, failure, and doubt, but there's something else too: **purpose**. *A life that felt like its own.*

That kind of clarity doesn't come from escaping the world, it grows when you turn inward and ask honest questions. You begin to see what truly matters, what sustains you, and what silently drains you. And yes, this isn't about cutting yourself off from people. It's about learning the difference between what nourishes your future and what you pursue just to feel accepted. The more honest you are with yourself, the easier it becomes to set boundaries without guilt and move through life without resentment.

Don't let the fear of judgment silence your truth. Each experience, whether it lifts you or tests you is a chance to grow. Learn to face mistakes without shame, rejection without losing hope, and failure without giving up on yourself.

The world doesn't need a version of you that blends in—it needs the version that's real, honest, imperfect, but true. That's why choosing self-respect over people-pleasing matters. When you trade your voice for comfort or your values for approval, it might feel easier for a while, but over time, it leaves you disconnected from yourself.

Success doesn't appear overnight. It's the result of showing up for consistently, patiently, even when progress feels invisible. Becoming who you truly are takes courage, especially the courage to keep going without shortcuts.

There will be days when you feel stuck or uncertain, when growth feels invisible and doubts get louder. That's part of the process too. Real change rarely looks dramatic—it happens quietly, in the choices you make when no one's watching.

You don't need to have it all figured out. You don't need to be perfect. What matters is that you stay engaged in your growth with presence, not pressure. The version of you today might differ from yesterday and that isn't failure, it's learning. Self-acceptance isn't about settling; it's about shedding the masks so real growth can begin.

If you want clarity, give yourself space. Reflect. Be still. Not every question needs an immediate answer. Some of the most profound shifts happen when you stop chasing and start listening.

<u>Here are few reminders to hold close:</u>

- **Be Real:** Your uniqueness matters more than anything you could compare in this world.
- **Social Media Trap:** What you see online is a curated version of someone's life. The bigger truth stays behind the scenes. Never confuse their snapshot with your own journey.
- **Let Go of Approval:** Societal opinions are unpredictable. If you chase praise, you will keep

reshaping yourself. Let your choices rise from your values instead of someone else's expectations.

- **Redefine Success:** Success is not measured by what you own; it is shaped by how you live.
- **Stay Rooted:** There will be moments when your beliefs feel tested. Never lose sight of your authentic self. Growth often begins in the moments that feel uncomfortable.
- **Know Yourself:** Give time to understand your thoughts, feelings, and habits. When you know yourself better, your decisions become clearer and your path feels more steady.
- **Keep Growing:** Life is a journey of continuous self-discovery. Keep learning, exploring new perspectives, and evolving as a person. This leads to deeper fulfilment.
- **Build Self-Love:** Treat yourself with care. When life feels heavy, self-love becomes the strength that keeps you steady.

No matter how loud/messy the world becomes, keep listening to yourself. The more you align with what's true within, the less you'll crave validation from outside. That truth will matter most when life tests you. Challenges will come—distractions too. Moments that questions your clarity, your patience, your direction. Each one is a reminder of telling you: **return to yourself.**

Sometimes you may need space from others to find yourself more clearly. And though it may feel hard, it often deepens your relationships in the long run. This is the Law of understanding yourself. And it's worth doing not just for peace, but for freedom.

Above all, value your growth, not for recognition, but for your own becoming. The more you accept and understand yourself, the more naturally you can offer real connection to others.

Choose with care. Let your past be a place of learning, not regret. And write a life your future self will look back on—not with shame, but with pride. A life that lets you smile and say, ***Yes, I made it.***

Message to my little sister

Dear Sister!

I wrote this book with you in mind every step of the way, driven by a burning desire to help you understand how the world will treat you in every season of your life. You never know when a loved one will betray you, when a friend will show their true colors, or when family will bring you tears. Everything changes with the seasons— *the good turns bad, and the bad turns good.* That is why; I want you to have as much knowledge as possible to navigate this unpredictable world.

My hope is for you to understand each season's rhythm so you can enjoy life's journey without being overwhelmed by its crises. Life will serve you many experiences—some bitter, like betrayal and disappointment, and others sweet, like love and victory. I want you to recognize each one as it comes, savoring the good and managing the bad.

I don't want you to be shocked when life throws you a curveball. If a friend betrays you, I want you to smile and say, **"Oh, I knew this might happen,"** and walk away untouched, like dust that never clings to your feet.

My greatest wish is for you to gain the power of knowledge, so you can choose your path in life rather than letting life choose it for you. When life chooses your path, it's often filled with confusion, pain, and disappointment. But when you choose your path, it's paved with clarity, peace, and victory.

To help you achieve this, I've poured my heart and experiences into this book. It's my hope that it will guide you through life's seasons and equip you with the wisdom to make informed decisions.

My only intention in writing this book is for you to gain as much knowledge and wisdom as possible, empowering you to face life's challenges with grace and strength.

My dearest little sister, I hope you embrace this opportunity to learn and grow wiser by reading this book.

Love from brother.

Head 

(Message)

Page: 21-44 [0.1—10]

Message 0.1

Fall in love with knowledge.

Don't confine yourself to the knowledge you already possess; you never know what the world has in store for you. One day your friends might turn back on you, or the one that you're close with may suddenly change their behaviour towards you. Lots of surprises and opportunities await you, and the key to unlocking them successfully is by continuously expanding your knowledge and skill set.

Life, in its own way, have cruelty and fleeting grace, offers both open hands and closed doors. And in that dance of fortune and failure, the only true compass is your ability to grow. Knowledge, like a lantern at dusk, must be kept lit, fed by curiosity, not comfort.

The future moves in silence, unfolding in ways no heart can predict. Today, a friend may carry your burdens as if they were their own; tomorrow, they might be the ones who place stones in your path. A partner who once embraced you with warmth might later confess that their affection was only an echo, not a vow. Love, too, can sometimes wear a mask.

Even family, those who once held your hand when you could not stand might unknowingly pull you away from your true path, urging you toward dreams that are not yours to dream. What begins as protection can become an unseen chain.

It is often those closest to us who teach us the most painful truths. Betrayal and disappointment arrive not from enemies, but from the familiar yet they shape us, if we let them. This is why you must let learning become your anchor. Let wisdom be the fire that does not flicker when the winds of uncertainty howl.

Never let your curiosity die. Seek not just answers, but deeper questions. Let knowledge be your silent ally, one that walks with you through every storm.

The more you learn, the less you cling; anchored not in promises, but in presence; not in others, but in the steady strength of your own becoming.

Message 0.2

Don't Silence the Child Within.

Growing up isn't easy, is it?

Back then, our worries fit inside a schoolbag, forgotten homework, a lost pencil, the slow-ticking clock before recess. **Now?** Adulthood hands us an invisible backpack, stuffed with *shoulds* and *what-ifs*. And somewhere along the way, we traded our treasures for tasks.

We zip it shut over monsoon afternoons when we ran barefoot through puddles, laughter as muddy water splashed up our legs; never once worrying the rain might bring a cold and over nights when we waited beneath blankets, eyes wide with wonder, eager for bedtime stories, those small joys, now shelved like outgrown shoes.

But time moves, and so do we. Somewhere between *"act your age"* and *"be responsible,"* we bury that spark. We trade curiosity for checklists, play for productivity. And slowly, almost unknowingly, life becomes quieter inside us. But a life without wonder is a clock without hands: you feel the ticking, but never the time.

We get one life. Why spend it kneeling at the altar of *'enough'*? Yes, carry the backpack, but leave room for fireflies and dreams. When we silence that inner child, we don't grow up. We just shrink down.

So let's remember what we once knew so easily that joy doesn't need permission, and wonder isn't something we outgrow. Be the kind of adult who names the clouds, who lets a sunset steal the last word, who knows laughter doesn't need an alibi. Growing up isn't about letting go of that child; it's about learning how to carry her with intention.

Your inner child is your strength and your sight—**the compass that once found magic in rain and still knows how to follow joy.** Carry her not as a memory, but as your guide.

Message 0.3

Not Every Story Is Ours to Tell

We all know someone who often speaks about others not out of malice, perhaps, but from a place they haven't yet healed. They share stories that weren't theirs to tell, focusing on people's flaws, failures, or moments of weakness. At first, it seems harmless, until you feel the heaviness it leaves behind.

What feels like harmless curiosity often becomes a quiet habit, one that slowly weaves itself into your pattern you never meant to be part of. At first, it feels like you're simply listening, staying polite, part of the moment. But something inside you begins to tighten. The more the conversation turns toward someone else's life, the more distant you feel from your own centre.

Without realizing it, you're drawn into a flow of judgment that doesn't sit right with your spirit. Instead of feeling closer, you walk away unsettled questioning not just what was said, but why you stayed.

Gossip is a bandage for the unhealed wounds, a quick fix that never sticks. Often, those who speak of others are just avoiding the mirror. It's easier to point at shadows than face your own light. And while it doesn't excuse the behavior, it does remind us: everyone is fighting a battle we can't always see.

That's why it matters so much to stay awake to the energy we allow around us. Not in fear, but in love; for our own peace and for the kind of presence we want to bring into the world.

You don't have to shame or correct them. Just quietly step back. *A tongue that keeps wounding others forgets how to taste grace.* Choose instead to be someone who listens with care, speaks with kindness, and protects what's sacred even in someone else's absence.

The people we choose to keep close shape us often more than we realize. So choose those who inspire growth, who talk about ideas, dreams, and healing—not the private lives of others. And when the moment comes where you feel tempted to join in, pause. Ask yourself gently: **Is this who I want to be?** Every conversation is an invitation to rise a little higher, to root a little deeper, and to become someone more grounded and true.

Protect your peace, not out of pride, but out of deep respect for the person you're becoming.

It's better to build your own character than to pick apart someone else's.

Message 0.4

We Don't Own the Morning, but We Do Have This Moment

Sometimes, life stops us mid-step. On my way to the office, I saw a small crowd gathered by the roadside. Some of them taking pictures, others watching intently, and two or three were on their phones making calls. One woman sat on the curb, weeping as if her whole world had caved in.

I moved closer, heart heavy with questions, and there he was a man lying still, blood pooling gently beneath his head. Nearby, a bike lay twisted, its front wheel turned inward like a broken wrist. A car stood a few paces away, its windshield shattered, its bumper crumpled like a crushed breath.

In that still, suspended moment, I realized how fragile life is, how quickly everything can end.

That man didn't know the morning would betray him. He left home with a routine in his mind, perhaps a destination, perhaps a dream. He didn't get to say goodbye. No final call. No last words. Just an ordinary moment that became the end of everything.

We live as if we have time. We postpone joy, delay forgiveness, silence our desire, and tell ourselves, *"someday or one-day."* But life is not a promise; we never know when our times will end. So live not recklessly, but deeply, boldly, and kindly. Live in a way that honors you and the life that makes you whole.

Chase what mends you not what simply fills your calendar. Say what needs to be said. Love without holding back. And walk away from anything that dims your light or silences your spirit.

You don't owe the world; you owe yourself your truth. Don't wait for the perfect time, make this time perfect by being fully in it.

Kiss your life not just one good day, but even when it trembles. Hold it close. For you only get one and no one knows how many mornings it has left.

Message 0.5

The Quiet Art of Letting Go

We've all made our share of mistakes, some we speak of, and some we keep tucked away, hoping time will soften their edges, all deeply human. Yet too often, we fall into the trap of clinging to the past dwelling on what went wrong, regretting our actions, and allowing those moments to define who we are. Instead of drawing wisdom from our missteps, we let them cast shadows over our present. We bury our heads in negative thinking and self-blame missing out on the joy and beauty unfolding before us. It's as if we've silently decided that our happiness no longer matters. We let the ghosts of past mistakes haunt us, robbing us of today's opportunities. And tomorrow, we'll blame ourselves again for not embracing the chances life so generously offered.

Oh, what a tragedy it is to let yesterday steal the light of today!

Tell me, who walks this earth without a misstep? Show me someone untouched by error, and I'll show you a soul that's never dared to live. Mistakes are not proof of failure, they're part of what makes us human: there is no shame in stumbling, in breaking, in moments of weakness. The real shame lies in refusing to learn, in shrinking from growth, in choosing to stay down when life calls us to rise.

Oh, what a shame it will be if we don't take the opportunity!

Learning is a part of life with every mistake; we're offered the chance to evolve. Each time, we stand at a crossroads: to remain bound by regret or to move forward with courage and grace. We can choose to live imprisoned by the past, or we can choose to meet each moment with an open mind and a forgiving heart.

Oh, what a beautiful life awaits those who dare to let go of their past!

Action is the gateway to growth. When we do nothing, we learn nothing. Growth does not come from perfection, but from motion. When we take risks, mistakes are inevitable, yet they become our greatest teachers. By embracing our flaws and failures, we free ourselves from the weight of regret and step boldly into the present.

Oh, what wisdom lies in learning, in letting go, in choosing to live fully and freely!

Message 0.6

Be the Butterfly in the Room

Our days brim with unpredictability. Each day brings moments that shape us, test us, and remind us of how human we are. In all that noise, what we often need most is a pause to return to ourselves, to steady the mind and protect our peace.

We step into different social spaces every day, often balancing our private truths with public masks. In a world that keeps telling us to do more and stay ahead, it is easy to drift into gossip. A small remark, a quick glance, a shared secret that feels like connection but leaves nothing meaningful behind.

Deep down, we know it never leads anywhere good. Pulling someone down does not lift us up. It does not bring peace—not the kind that lasts. Real peace grows from within. In the moments when we choose patience even when judgment feels tempting, in the grace we offer when it would be simpler to criticize. In the choice to stay kind when the world feels heavy.

We were made for more—we have purpose. So why give energy to anything that dims your light.

<u>Let this guide you:</u>

- *True beauty doesn't bloom in criticism.*
- *Respect is never rooted in judgment.*
- *And real intelligence? It rises above the noise.*

Gossip shrinks the room we're in. It dims the very light we bring. The more we engage in it, the more it reshapes us, not those we speak of. But when we choose empathy instead, we become the light. We build trust, create space, and offer others something rare: **safety.**

So choose with care. Speak with intention. Let your words build bridges, not walls. Let them reflect the best of who you are, and the life you're creating.

**Be the butterfly in the room. Spread wings of positivity, and let the world see your light.*

Message 0.7

Comparison Is the Thief of Your Own Beauty

You were never meant to be anyone else; you are one flower among many, blooming in your own way.

The world's beauty defies imagination; every moment brims with wonder and admiration. When you open your eyes, you're greeted by the marvels that surround you. When you listen closely, you'll hear the symphony of life, its melodies and harmonies captivating your soul. The fragrances carried on the breeze can transport you to distant memories and realms. Yet, amidst all this beauty, we often forget to appreciate what we already have.

Your friend buys new clothes from a luxury brand, and while you admire their style, you overlook the value of your own wardrobe. They drive a new car, and while you envy their purchase, you dismiss the reliability of your own. You scroll through social media, admiring the curated lives of others, and let a highlight reel dictate your worth. In constantly comparing yourself to others, you fail to see the unique blessings that are already yours. Your body is not a trending topic. Your joy is not a viral algorithm. Stop waiting for external validation to render you in high resolution.

What a shame it is to live in a world so full of beauty, yet be blind to the treasures within ourselves. Isn't it odd that we inhabit these bodies, these lives, and yet seek validation from external sources instead of appreciating what we already possess? Imagine giving someone a gift, only for them to compare it to what others have received and dismiss your generosity. How would that make you feel?

When someone gives you something, the natural response is gratitude. Similarly, when life blesses you, the healthiest response is appreciation. Trace the miracles that shape your day; each one holds its own unique value, contributing to the richness of your life. And when you begin to notice these gifts, you'll find that gratitude doesn't just comfort—it transforms.

So choose to see the beauty in your own story. Honor your journey, resist the urge to measure it against another's, and remember: one of the greatest acts of self-love is simply recognizing the worth that was always yours.

The world hands you funhouse mirrors; distorted, flattering, cracked, and then asks why you don't recognize yourself. So hold onto what's real. *Cherish the way your life blooms-uniquely, without needing to compete.* **Let others chase the spotlight. You stay close to your own flame.** And when you forget, come back here. Come back to yourself. You were never meant to be anyone else.

"The thief of your beauty is not time, its comparison."

Message 0.8

The Ones Who Carry Your Story

Stay away from people who praise you in public yet criticize you when you are not around.

Not everyone who claps for you is in your corner. Some will cheer when you're winning, but go questions your ability when you're not in the room. A true friend, one who speaks your name with respect even when you're not around is worth more than a thousand admirers who only love you when it benefits them.

It's easy to get caught up in people's attention. The flattery, the messages, the feeling of being seen—it feels good. Yet not every hand that applauds you holds you up. Some people are opportunists. They'll lift you up when there's something in it for them… and disappear the moment they've taken what they came for. Be careful not to lose someone real chasing after something that never was.

A real friend won't flatter you to keep you happy. They'll tell you the truth, even if it's uncomfortable. They'll stand up for you without needing to be asked. And they won't need an audience to do it. Their loyalty doesn't come with a spotlight; it comes with time, trust, and trust alone.

And yet, in moments of pride or restlessness, we sometimes overlook them. We trade deep roots for quick applause. We drift toward people who seem exciting, forgetting the ones who've quietly had our back through every version of ourselves. But what looks like gold on the surface can leave you hollow underneath.

Think about the people who know your mess and never made you feel small for it. Who didn't walk away when you were difficult to love. That kind of presence is rare. That kind of love is steady, like a hand on your back when you're tired of holding yourself up.

So if you've got someone like that in your life, don't take them for granted. Don't let a shallow moment cost you something sacred. You don't need to explain yourself to everyone. But you do owe your loyalty to the ones who never asked you to be perfect to stay.

And when you're tempted by the thrill of being liked, pause and ask yourself: *who stood by me when no one was watching?* That's who matters. In the end, it's not the people who praised you that you'll remember. It's the ones who stayed.

Flattery is cheap. Loyalty costs time.

Message 0.9

<u>Before We Call It Love</u>

"Love begins in feeling, but survives in understanding."

Not every flutter in the heart is a signal to begin. Feelings may bloom like wildflowers after rain, sudden and beautiful, but not every field is meant to be harvested. Lots of beauty may come into our lives; unexpected, stirring, even unforgettable, but allure alone is not a reason to remain. Some moments are meant to be witnessed, not held. Some souls are like seasons, they are meant to pass through us, not take root.

We must choose love the way a gardener chooses a seed, not just for its bloom, but for the patience it requires, the understanding it demands, and the seasons it must survive.

When we choose to love someone, we begin to build, slowly, gently. Layer by layer, we shape something shared. Not to keep the world out, but to hold a world we create together. But here's what many forget: before we lay the first stone, there must be clarity. **Understanding is the map; without it, we are only wandering with someone, not walking toward something.**

A relationship is not born from feelings alone. Feelings are the spark, *"yes,"* but understanding is the foundation. Without it, love becomes a house with no ground beneath it: beautiful for a moment, but always one storm away from collapse.

So before you call it love, pause. See them, not as you wish them to be, but as they are. Ask: *Do I understand this soul I am about to anchor mine to? Do we share direction, or only desire?* **Because love, real love, is not just how we feel, it's what we're willing to build.**

Message 10

<u>Joy Is Freedom, Wisdom Is the Way.</u>

"The beauty of life is not in the destination; it lies in the journey that lets you feel everything on the path."

Go on; wear the mascara, apply the foundation, make plans that make your heart glow. Dine out with your friends; Laugh loudly in cafés where memories are made, not just meals. Let joy find you, even in the middle of a Monday.

And to the brothers—pack that bag; let's chase the winds. Take that late-night ride with music too loud and hearts wide open. Sit beneath glowing evenings, speak your truths, and hold your people close.

We get one life. Just one. And this moment. It's a moment we owe ourselves. A gift to be lived, not merely survived. Still, living fully asks for more than feeling deeply. Not every storm is calmed by emotion alone.

Fun is freedom, but wisdom is direction. And direction comes not from impulse, but from knowing, from choosing, from listening to what's greater than us. Knowledge begins in humility and true wisdom grows only when we learn to listen.

So laugh, live, and leap, but plant your feet where the future awaits. Every choice is a seed. Some grow into shade, others into thorns. What we water today decides what we will one day stand beneath.

Body

Page: [45-218]

<----------------------------------->

Index

This index lets you directly jump to the page you want to read.

When you learn to rest in your own heart, you draw the right people toward you.

Love yourself

The deepest gift you can offer the world is the love you first pour into yourself. No one—not even the ones who adore you can carry the weight of your dream but you.

Your life is shaped not by the love you seek from others, but by the love and belonging you nurture within yourself. No one knows you the way you do. Others may care, they may offer moments of comfort or flashes of understanding, but they cannot fully grasp the landscape of your soul, nor can they carry the weight of your desires.

It's a comforting illusion to believe someone else can complete us. At times, those closest to us; friends, family, partners do offer genuine love and support. But even their presence, though meaningful, is not enough to sustain us in the long run. What endures is the relationship you build with yourself, the one marked by compassion, acceptance, and clarity. No matter how much love you receive from others, it will never be enough if you are estranged from your own self.

One truth I've come to understand, often through pain, is that no one can fulfil my deepest desires, nor can I fully fulfil theirs. No matter how much love I pour into the people I care about, there's always seems to be a gap between what they hope for and what I can give. I've seen it time and again: I offer something with love, and it brings them brief joy… but soon comes the next expectation, the next unspoken demand. And when I fall short, their disappointment becomes mine to carry.

The same has been true in reverse. I've searched for someone who could understand the unspoken corners of my heart, someone who could see and meet my needs without explanation, but such understanding never truly came. The reality is, no one else can access the depths of my being but me. My struggles, my longings, my inner silence, these are mine to carry alone, even those who seems to love me has no key to unlock my burden. And that is not their fault. It's simply the nature of being human.

At times, this realization feels heavy. It feels like lighting a lantern in a fog, hoping someone sees it, but the mist just swallows the flame. But when I think deeply or connected to the reality of nature: I am the only one who can truly hear myself. I am the only one who can meet my own needs, tend to my wounds, and build a home within my soul.

So, learn to stand by yourself. Nurture the parts of you that long to be seen. Invest in your well-being, not as an act of selfishness, but as a sacred responsibility. Let your energy flow into the things that bring you peace and purpose. Don't waste your days trying to be everything to everyone; live so fully and sincerely that others are inspired by your wholeness, not your sacrifice.

In the end, your life is yours alone. And when you honour that truth, you become not just self-sufficient, but radiant; with a love that does not need to be begged for, because it already lives inside you.

So ask yourself:

- If you can love someone deeply, can you also learn to love yourself with the same devotion?
- If you can forgive others for their mistakes, can you extend that forgiveness to your own heart?
- If you can be kind to someone else, can you offer that kindness to the person in the mirror?
- If you can make peace with others, can you sit with your past and make peace with yourself?
- If you can sacrifice your time for others, can you also prioritize your own well-being, without guilt?

There is nothing more essential than learning to care for yourself, to tend to your inner garden before offering its flowers to others. You are the only one who can feel the shape of your longings, the weight of your unmet needs, the kind of love that doesn't just soothe, but sustains.

Before building a relationship with anyone, build one with yourself; honest, compassionate, and whole. Only then can love become something you give freely, not something you trade for approval or security.

We've all heard the phrase, *"You cannot pour from an empty cup."* I once understood it as a metaphor. Now, I know it as a reality.

I remember a moment in Dec 2022. I had just come from a job interview—hopeful but exhausted, unemployed, and uncertain. As I walked out of the Metro station, I saw a little girl curled near the stairs. Her clothes were torn, her skin exposed to the bitter cold. She looked up and, through chattering lips, whispered, *"Bhaiya... maine subah se kuchh nahi khaya... mujhe kuchh khila do."* (*Brother... I haven't eaten since morning. Please give me something to eat.*)

My heart broke, but my wallet was empty. I had barely enough for my own way home.

In that moment, I realised the deep pain of wanting to help but not being able to. It wasn't a lack of compassion; it was a lack of capacity.

That moment etched something deep within me. I realized that good intentions are not enough; you must be *equipped* to act on them. If I had money, I would've fed her. If I had strength, I would've stood by her. But because I hadn't yet built a life where I could care for myself, I couldn't care for her either.

The same applies to emotional and spiritual abundance. When we are empty, tired, broken, disconnected. We cannot offer others what we do not have. Trying to give from a place of lack is like attempting to solve an equation where both sides are zero; there is nothing to divide, nothing to give, no answer that can bring light.

So invest in yourself, not as an act of selfishness, but of preparation. Fill your cup so that it may overflow. Heal your heart so that it can become a place of shelter for others. Love yourself, so that your love for others is not dependency, but a gift.

We can do nothing when we have nothing

We can't offer what we don't have within. If our hearts are tired, if our minds are restless, if our cups are empty, what is left to give? That's why our first responsibility is toward ourselves: to care, to listen, and to truly understand what we need.

When we learn to love ourselves, not just in words, but in consistent action, we begin to refill what life has slowly drained. It's in those small acts of self-respect, of choosing rest, of honoring our boundaries, that we slowly gather strength again.

You can't help the poor if your own pockets are empty.
You can't offer clarity when your thoughts are clouded.
You can't heal others when your own wounds remain open.
And you can't love deeply if you haven't learned to be gentle with yourself.

This isn't selfishness; it's the foundation of everything we hope to give. Only when we are full within can we pour into others, not out of pressure or pretense, but from a place of truth, strength, and abundance.

So take the time to know yourself, to nourish your spirit, and to grow from within. The more you give yourself what you truly need, the more you'll have to share naturally, honestly, and with grace. That is where true generosity begins. And that is how a fulfilling life unfolds not all at once, but in steady steps, starting with you.

"Love begins in the place where you meet yourself with honesty."

You are the author of your life story. The plot, the subject, the tone it all begins and ends with you. No one else holds the pen. No one else can write your chapters or place a full stop on your journey. What unfolds on these pages is shaped by your thoughts, your actions, and the meaning you choose to give them.

You can learn from your mistakes. You can grow from your successes. You can gather insight from friends, family, or even strangers. But remember, they are not the main characters in your story. They are your references, not your script. Like a researcher sorting through sources, you decide what to keep, what to learn from, and what to let go. You don't need to include every detail. You don't need to carry everything forward.

Some days, you'll meet someone with a smile. The next day, that same person may greet you with silence or a storm. Today, your emotions may rise with joy; tomorrow, they may fall with tears. Today, a lover may give you roses; tomorrow, they may hand you heartbreak. People, events, emotions, they are all moments. They are not the story itself. They are just parts of the unfolding chapters that teach, test, and transform.

So don't hold them too tightly. Don't blame them, and don't let them define your worth. Reflect on them, be inspired by them, but always remember:

the story is yours to write.

Keep writing honestly, bravely, and with grace.
And if ever you wonder who's holding the pen...
Just look in the mirror. The most powerful author of
your life has always been you.

The facts remain the same for everyone. What changes is the way we see them, and through that vision, the meaning we give to our experiences. A single moment can feel like a burden or a lesson, a setback or a turning point, depending on the lens we carry within us. That is why perspective matters. Choose how you see with care, so you do not mistake a chapter for a conclusion or misread the story you are still living.

Beware Those Who Always Find Fault

"A single mind can turn a paradise into a prison."

It was one of those golden mornings in March; soft sunlight spilling over the mountains, warming our faces as we sat with coffee cups nestled between our palms. The kind of morning that feels quiet, familiar, and full of unspoken peace. We were at our usual corner café, just a few friends easing into the day with conversation and caffeine. But that morning took a different turn. One of my friends brought his cousin along a new face, unfamiliar energy. And from the moment he joined us, the atmosphere shifted.

He introduced himself with a smile, but what followed wasn't a warm hello, it was a monologue. Within minutes, he hijacked the conversation, barely letting anyone else speak. He brags about the many cities he had visited, listing them like trophies. But instead of sharing the beauty or the charm of these places, he focused only on what was wrong the food, the people, the chaos, the discomfort. His words dripped with disdain, not experience.

Among the cities he mentioned was Manipur; a land nestled in the northeastern hills of India, known for its lush green valleys, vibrant festivals, and rich tribal culture. Picture the serene Loktak Lake shimmering under the morning sun, the graceful hills dotted with wild orchids, including the rare and exquisite Shirui Lily blossoming in the mist, and the inviting aroma of local spices filling the air. But to him, it was just another place of inconvenience and disappointment.

We listened. Silently. Some of us exchanged glances—you know the kind that says, *"Are you hearing this too?"* But we said nothing, because, well, he was a guest. All we could do was sip our coffee and try to redirect the conversation, though his negativity always found a way to dominate.

That morning left a strange taste. Bitter, not because of the coffee, but because of how heavy someone's energy can be when it's laced with constant criticism. It reminded me how much of a person's character is revealed not by what they say, but by how they choose to say it.

"You can choose to talk about the thorns of the roses, or you can choose to talk about their beauty. It is the choice we make that tells us who we are."

Later that week, I spoke with a friend who had visited Manipur. She described it as if it were a dream; the calm expanse of Loktak Lake, the delicate Shirui Lily blooming on the hillsides, the grace of traditional dance performances, the genuine warmth of the local people, and the rich, tantalizing aroma of indigenous cuisine. Her eyes lit up as she spoke, and I found myself wanting to experience the place for myself.

Here is the twist!

Same city, Different stories. What changed? Not Manipur itself, but the storyteller.

I'm not here to say one is right and the other is wrong. But I do believe how we choose to tell our stories says more about us than about the places or people we talk about.

There's a lesson in that; a reminder that our perception often shapes our reality far more than the reality itself. Two people can experience the same place, the same moment, and come away with completely different stories because they carry different minds, hearts, and attitudes. How we choose to see the world influences how we live in it. And more importantly, it influences how others experience us. Choosing to focus on negativity can trap us in a cycle of dissatisfaction, while choosing to see the beauty, even amidst flaws, opens doors to growth, connection, and joy.

Just because someone is well-traveled doesn't mean they are wise. Just because someone speaks confidently doesn't mean they understand deeply. And just because someone had a bad experience doesn't make their perspective the only truth.

Some people walk into a room and lift it. Others dim the light the moment they speak. The difference often lies not in the world they've seen, but in the world they carry inside.

So if you ever meet someone who only points out what's broken, pause and ask yourself, are they describing the world, or unconsciously revealing the wounds they carry inside? Because sometimes, what spills out from their lips is less about the places they've been, and more about the shadows they haven't yet faced.

At the end of the day, it's not about judging others as good or bad. It's about observing with clarity. If someone's energy doesn't align with yours, you don't have to fix them. You don't have to argue. You simply step back, learn what you can, and keep your peace.

Be the person who sees the light in the room even when others focus on the shadows. Choose to carry warmth, to lift quietly, and to bring hope where it's needed most.

Note: *Be careful with the people who love finding negative things about others. Today they enjoyed sharing negative things about others in front of you tomorrow in your absence you become the subject of their negative discussions.*

Life moves through every thought you hold and every choice you make. What you nurture within gradually shapes the direction of your days and how heavy or light life feels as you move forward. When you learn to guide your mind with care, your actions begin to align with what truly matters to you. From that alignment, purpose does not need to be searched for. It reveals itself through the way you live.

Avoid negative thoughts.

Life delivers unseen challenges daily, yet it is the courage in our choices that decides who we become.

Our thoughts are seeds; we harvest what we plant. A kind mind bears kind fruit, while bitterness breeds only thorns. No matter the storm outside, we still hold the compass of perception. We can choose how we see through clarity or confusion, with openness or resistance. The situation may not be in our hands, but the meaning we assign to it always is.

Yet, many of us hope for joy while planting seeds of despair. We feed our minds with negativity, then wonder why the harvest is barren. Expecting peace while nursing resentment is like expecting a torch to shine without ever placing the batteries inside. Light does not arrive without intention. Nor do positive outcomes without positive thoughts. Our inner world shapes how we interpret the outer one. When we shift our thoughts, our experiences follow. A change in mindset is often the first step toward a change in reality. When we choose to focus on the good, we begin to weave a more fulfilling life; thread by thread, thought by thought.

Take something as simple as a camping trip in the mountains. Of course, there may be bugs, a lack of clean water, no proper restroom, and a fair share of discomfort. But that's not the whole story. There's also the hush of the night sky, the stillness of pine trees, the fire's gentle crackle, the wind whispering in silence, and the feeling of being wrapped in the arms of nature. If we dwell only on the inconveniences, we miss the wonder that's waiting to unveil. Joy doesn't require a perfect setting, it requires a willing mind. Sometimes, to find beauty, we must look past the discomfort.

If your thoughts stay tethered to the negative, your experience will echo that tone. But if you let gratitude, openness, and patience guide you, even a rough path can feel like a meaningful journey. There's a quote that comes to mind, though perhaps it's been said in many forms: *"A wise soul sees the glass half full not because they ignore the empty, but because they choose to honour what is still there."* Perspective, after all, is not just a point of view; it's a way of life.

Beneath it all, one truth remains: where your thoughts go, your life follows. Speak gently to your mind, feed it well, and it will lead you somewhere beautiful.

Don't be a slave to your negative self-perception

Thoughts are like passing strangers. Some knock gently, others storm the gates, but none can enter unless you let them in.

It's far too easy to slip into negative thoughts, to let the shadows grow louder than the light. And yet, the truth remains—your inner world is yours to guard. No one has the power to plant doubt or sorrow unless you let them in.

We often come across moments or experiences that feel out of sync with our desires. They stir discomfort, unease; sometimes anger. These aren't signs of weakness; they're whispers from within, gentle reminders that something around us doesn't sit right with what we truly desire. And that's okay. Feel them. Acknowledge their presence. But don't offer them a home. Let your conscious mind become the gatekeeper; sift through these thoughts with tenderness. If they hold no weight, let them pass like autumn leaves carried off by the wind. Not every thought deserves to take root in the garden of your mind.

After all, when you throw away garbage, you don't need to inspect it. You don't examine the texture or scent of something you're ready to release. In the same way, not every negative thought deserves your analysis. Some simply need to be discarded without question.

Focusing on what is good and true allows us to reclaim our power. The more we shift our gaze to the light, the less we are trapped by shadows. We are not meant to be servants to our doubts. We are meant to grow through them, not within them.

I remember October 2018, in the cool air of Dehradun, where we gathered for a youth camp nestled in the hills. I had the chance to speak one evening to share thoughts on something I believe deeply in: **the importance of setting**

boundaries in relationships. I spoke with clarity and heart, and I sensed the audience was engaged. It felt right.

But the next morning, one of the resource persons challenged my point openly, in front of everyone. He argued that boundaries can limit growth and potential. His words cut through me like a sharp wind. I felt my heart sink, and my mind filled with questions that echoed self-doubt: *Why did he say that? Was I wrong? Did I embarrass myself?*

For a while, those thoughts consumed me. I spiralled quietly and my confidence shaken by a single disagreement. But I took a moment. I let the storm in my head settle. Then I approached him not with confrontation, but with curiosity. We talked. We listened. And in the stillness of that conversation, we uncovered a simple truth: it was a misunderstanding. We weren't truly at odds—just speaking from different corners of the same room.

That moment taught me something lasting: words only have power when we allow them to live in us. The reactions we choose are our own creation. A comment, a disagreement, even a harsh tone, they're just passing winds. It is we who decide whether to build walls, raise sails, or stand still.

Beneath it all, one truth remains:

You are the gatekeeper of your inner world. Thoughts may knock, but they enter only when invited. No one's opinion can wound you unless you grant it permission. Reactions are choices, not chains. And in every moment, you are free to guard your peace, to welcome growth, and to let go of what does not belong.

Cultivate positive thoughts.

Everything begins in the mind. Before the journey, before the decision, before the word, there is thought. And that thought, whether drenched in fear or rooted in hope, sets the course for what follows. If you wish to change your life, you must begin where all change begins: in the silence of your thinking.

A positive mind is the quiet architect of a beautiful life. It doesn't command, it simply plants, nurtures, and lets bloom. What you think, you become. A single gentle thought of hope can stir an emotion, and that emotion, in turn, moves you toward meaningful action. It's a graceful cycle—thought becoming feeling, feeling becoming movement, and movement shaping reality.

Think of your mind as a garden. Positive thoughts are seeds of light, they need tending, patience, and care. With time, they grow into clarity, resilience, and joy. But if you let the weeds of doubt and fear take root, they crowd out what is beautiful. Left unchecked, they choke the life from your inner soil. As the old saying goes, *"Whether you think you can, or you think you can't, you're right."* The direction of your life begins in your thinking.

To change the world outside, you must begin with the world within. A mind grounded in beauty will inevitably reflect that beauty in its surroundings. When you choose to see through the lens of hope, you begin to notice doors where you once saw only walls. And when you confine your thoughts to what uplifts, rather than what drags you down, life quietly begins to open its arms.

The more you train your mind toward light, the more it becomes your natural resting place. This doesn't mean you deny the existence of pain, but you choose not to dwell there. You become the master of your inner dialogue, not its captive.

So nourish your thoughts. Meditate. Practice gratitude, even for small things. Surround yourself with people who lift rather than drain. Let your inner space be a sanctuary, not a battlefield. Because in the end, the mind is not just a mirror of the world, it's the hand that shapes the actions.

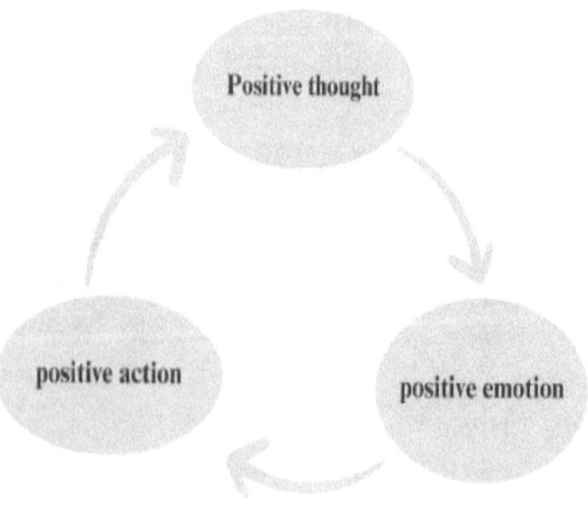

Meditation:

There are moments when the world grows loud, and the soul quietly asks for silence. **Meditation is not an escape, it is a return.** A return to the part of ourselves that remains untouched by chaos. In the stillness, we don't force the mind to stop moving; we simply learn to stop chasing it.

Each breath becomes a gentle anchor. Each pause, a space where peace can enter. Over time, we begin to recognize that the calm we seek was never outside, it was waiting within us, beneath the noise, beneath the clutter of constant thought.

To sit in silence is to remember who you are without the weight of the world pressing in. It is where clarity finds you not because you searched for it, but because you finally stopped running.

Gratitude:

Gratitude is a lens, not a list. It shifts the way we see— not by changing what we have, but by helping us see the fullness of what's already there. The more we give thanks, the more we begin to notice just how much beauty surrounds us in ordinary moments.

It's not about grand gestures. Sometimes it's as simple as feeling the warmth of morning light on your face, or recalling a kind word from someone who didn't have to say it. Gratitude transforms the mind and softens it. It replaces scarcity with sufficiency, and restlessness with joy.

Celebrate your progress, however small. Honour your efforts. Take yourself out, write yourself a note, light a candle. Let these be rituals of self-respect. When you affirm what is good in your life, you expand your capacity to receive more of it.

To feel grateful is to remember that life, even in its imperfection, is still a gift.

Surround yourself with positive people

A nourishing environment is not a luxury; it's a form of self-respect.

The people we surround ourselves with are like mirrors, we begin to reflect their energy, their words, their worldview. Without realizing it, their presence begins to shape our perception of what is possible, acceptable, and true.

If you often find yourself in the company of those who dwell in complaint, who find joy in criticism or cynicism, it becomes harder to hear your own inner optimism. But when you're around those who speak with kindness, who celebrate growth, who choose hope even on difficult days, you begin to rise with them.

Energy is contagious. So choose carefully. Seek out souls who remind you of your worth, who water your dreams, not your doubts. Surround yourself with those who make you feel lighter, not lesser.

Avoid negative self-talk.

We all have days when the weight of the world seems to press a little harder on our shoulders, when doubt drips quietly into our thoughts, and negativity begins to whisper louder than hope. If left unchallenged, these thoughts do more than linger; they become lodgers in our minds, distorting how we see ourselves and dimming the light of our own potential.

During the final year of my graduation, I found myself drowning in deadlines and dread. Assignments piled like unscaled peaks. My project submission loomed just a week away and I hadn't even begun. Final semester exams lingered in the background like a second wave of pressure waiting to crash, and my books sat unopened. To make matters worse, I didn't have the financial means to conduct the fieldwork my project required. Everything felt like a tide rising too fast, and I was already knee-deep.

As the pressure mounted, so did the self-doubt. I questioned whether I could finish at all. It felt as though I had already failed, long before the exam papers were even printed. I blamed my past self for being too carefree, too lenient, too late. I told myself I deserved failure and for a moment, I believed it.

In that narrow, quiet space between panic and paralysis, my mind became a battleground. But amidst the turmoil, one truth flickered with quiet clarity: I had to try. Whether I passed or fell short, I owed myself the dignity of effort. So, I began.

With no budget and barely any time, I started piecing together my project, gathering fragments of information from the internet like a squirrel stashing acorns before winter. At night, with a cup of black coffee cradled between my hands, I became an owl, awake in the in the hush of the night, weaving research into coherence while the world slept.

I lived that way for over a week, a rhythm of survival and quiet determination, until my project was complete. I submitted it before the deadline, and somehow, I managed to prepare for and clear my exams. My graduation certificate may not shine as brightly as my peers', but for me, it represents something far more meaningful: a personal triumph.

In those ten frantic days, I didn't break a world record, but I broke a *belief*: the belief that I couldn't. And that shift was everything. People often spend months doing what I did in days, but I did it not with ease, and not without fear, but with resolve. That, in itself, made me feel like the hero of my own small story.

Looking back, I realize the real battle wasn't against the syllabus or the ticking clock. It was against my own mind. If I had listened to the voice that whispered "you can't," I would've never heard the one that whispered back, *"try."*

Our thoughts shape our path far more than we realize. If we treat every negative thought as gospel truth, we build walls where there could be doors. We see problems where solutions are waiting to be found. We give up before the first step is even taken.

Still, a quiet truth remains—we always have a choice. To reframe the way we think. To reclaim the narrative before it slips too far from who we are. We can let fear hold us hostage, or let courage, even if trembling guide our next step. Had I not challenged those inner shadows, I wouldn't have graduated, and perhaps more importantly, I wouldn't believe in myself the way I do now.

So don't let the voice of doubt define your story. Don't let it chain you to who you used to be. If you allow negativity to settle in, it will colonize your thoughts and convince you that you are powerless. It will steal your voice, your will, and your wonder.

That is why you must become the master of your mind. Speak to yourself not with judgment, but with belief. Replace *"I can't"* with *"I will try."* Replace fear with presence. Let your will rise louder than your worry.

In the end, it's not about being the best in the room; it's about showing up when it's hardest to. That is where real growth takes root. That is where victories are born, the kind that no one else sees, but that forever change the way you see yourself.

<u>**Positive thought in negative situations:**</u>

What if the heaviest weight you carry isn't your circumstances, but the thoughts you let settle in your mind?

We've all faced moments shadowed by negativity personally or professionally. Days when nothing seems to align, and even the smallest effort feels heavy. It's during these stretches that positive thinking becomes not only hardest to hold, but most needed.

When life turns against us, our minds can become our greatest saboteurs. One thought leads to another, and before we know it, we're spiraling into a space where everything feels dim. But even in the midst of that darkness, there's a quiet truth we often forget: we are not entirely at the mercy of our circumstances; we still have the power to choose how we respond to them.

Thoughts are not just visitors; they are architects. If we allow negative thoughts to settle, they begin shaping the very rooms we live in. But when we catch ourselves early—when we pause, breathe, and gently challenge what we're telling ourselves, we open a window. And sometimes, that's all it takes for a little light to come through.

It's much like the air we breathe. We don't choose the winds, but we can choose what we inhale. Why feed our minds polluted air when we have the choice to breathe in something cleaner, calmer, and clearer? Choosing positivity isn't pretending things are perfect, it's choosing a clearer lens, one that gives us the whole picture, not just the pain.

Reframing a negative situation doesn't mean pretending everything's okay. It simply means asking, *"What can I learn from this? Where can I grow?"* Often, that one question softens the edges of a hard day.

Let's say you're criticized harshly at work, maybe even fired for something you didn't fully understand. It would be easy to let that moment define you, to let embarrassment or anger build walls around you. But what if, instead, you saw it as a moment of redirection? An opportunity to deepen your skills, discover work that aligns more with your values, or even take the first step toward a new beginning? Negativity may shout, but it's still just one voice and you can choose to listen to another.

"A boat doesn't sink because of the water around it, but because of the water that gets in." The same is true for us. It's not the world outside that defeats us, it's what we let in, unguarded and unquestioned.

My father used to say, "It's not the matter that reacts to you, it's you who reacts to the matter." That one line stayed with me. Every situation carries a choice either to let it break us or shape us. And that choice begins in the mind. So the next time negativity knocks, pause before you answer. Ask, "Is this thought lifting me or weighing me down?" If it pulls you under, let it pass. Speak to yourself not with judgment, but with belief. Replace "This is the end" with "Maybe this is where something new begins."

What matters is not avoiding negativity altogether—that's not possible. It's about refusing to let it set the tone for your life. You may not command the storm, but you still hold the wheel. And sometimes, showing up with a clear mind and a steady heart—that alone is a quiet victory.

The impact of a positive mindset

They'll tell you change requires grand actions, but the real revolution begins in a single thought. It lays the foundation not only for finding solutions but also for perceiving life's challenges through a more generous and constructive lens. Where once we saw obstacles as immovable barriers, we begin to see them as doorways leading not to defeat, but to growth, to understanding, and to our own becoming.

This is where the heart of change truly lies—not in noise or spectacle, but in the silent, interior shift that reshapes how we see and respond to the world. Before any action is taken, before any plan is drawn, it is thought that lays the groundwork. And not just any thought, but one born of belief, of hope, of the quiet conviction that something better is possible.

To understand the inner power of positive thinking is to grasp one of life's simplest yet most essential truths. It does not promise a life without hardship, but it offers the strength to meet hardship with grace. It nourishes confidence, awakens clarity, and gives courage to walk the uncertain path.

Consider, for instance, a beautiful idea, perhaps a business vision that stirs your soul. If such a dream is shadowed by self-doubt and the fear of failure, even its brilliance may fade. Negative thoughts act like fog on a clear morning, blurring your steps and draining your resolve. But when you choose to believe in your potential—when you replace **"I can't"** with **"I can,"** the contours of your dream begin to take shape. Possibility returns.

This single shift, the moment we choose belief over fear, is not just powerful; it is transformative. Thought does more than reflect our world—it colors it, shapes it, even redefines what we believe is possible. When we begin to nourish thoughts that strengthen rather than shrink us, we awaken a current within that gently, yet persistently, carries us toward the life we long for.

Acceptance, too, is part of this subtle strength. Change and uncertainty are woven into the very rhythm of life like day and night, sorrow and joy. To resist them is to struggle against the tide; to embrace them with a steady heart is to learn how to float, to adapt, to grow. Even hardship, when seen with open eyes, holds within it the seeds of wisdom.

Let us remember: every experience, whether gentle or jarring, carries a lesson meant to shape us. Growth does not ask for perfection; it asks only for presence, for willingness, for belief. A positive mindset does not deny reality; it simply refuses to be defeated by it.

So when the weight of the world leans heavy, remember: the thought you choose today is the first step through a doorway you cannot yet see. Behind it lies not just a way forward, but the very self you are becoming; one who builds bridges from barriers, who carves light from the fog. The obstacles? They were never walls. They were the raw material of your courage. And the door? It was yours to open all along.

<u>**Recap**</u>:

Negative thoughts are like passing clouds; they drift in, but they don't have to define the sky. In any situation, the first step is to pause and observe them without judgment, recognizing them as fleeting mental events rather than absolute truths. Instead of feeding them, gently redirect your attention to what is constructive, present, and within your control. Ground yourself in the moment, and remind yourself that your perception shapes your reality more than the circumstances themselves.

We spend much of our lives chasing versions of life shaped by others' expectations, comparisons, and ideals. In that pursuit, we slowly drift away from our own inner voice. Clarity does not arrive through speed or imitation. It appears when we turn inward, and give ourselves the space to listen. That inward meeting is where understanding begins, and where your own life starts to grow.

Be you.

Be yourself and stay true to your core values; stop losing yourself in the mirror of others

Every day, the world tells you who to be. But when you trade authenticity for approval, you begin living under the mercy of their shadow.

The world starts shaping your thoughts before you're even fully awake. Half-awake, your hand reach instinctively for the phone. A cascade of notifications awaits, each one tugging you further from your own centre. As you scroll through curated lives and filtered smiles, silently a comparison begins. Unseen but deeply felt, it seeps in. You feel it in the pressure to keep up, to match, to matter even before your day really begins. And just like that, the rhythm of your morning is no longer your own.

Later, you're out with friends for a walk. You notice their clothes, the way they talk, how confident they seem. And suddenly, a bit of self-doubt slips in. You start questioning your own choices, your outfit, your energy, your presence. Then, as you pass a coffee shop, you notice a woman who stands out confident, composed, bold red lips, effortless style. In your mind, she becomes the new standard. And before you can stop it, the thought arises: *I wish I looked like her.*

Further down the street, a sleek car pulls up. A well-dressed man steps out, looking like he has everything figured out. Without meaning to, your thoughts drift again *"What if my partner looked like that?" "What if my life did?"*

Bit by bit, you absorb these outside images. And without realizing it, you start losing touch with what matters to you—your values, your truth, your sense of enough. Approval from others starts to matter more than peace with yourself. You begin looking outward for answers, instead of inward. Your reflection becomes something you search for in the eyes of others.

Pause and ask yourself:

- *Who will look out for you if you keep reshaping yourself just to fit in?*
- *Who fills your emotional space when you keep chasing outside validation?*
- *Who defines your worth if you never give yourself the chance to?*

You begin letting go of your real self-piece by piece and instead, try to become someone who looks more like *them.* You chase images, not truth. And it's exhausting. Like a fish dreaming of walking on land, you end up far from your own self, unsure of who you are anymore.

But just because the world is loud doesn't mean you have to lose your voice. The world is full of colours and you are among those one colour. While you're busy admiring others, someone out there may be admiring you quietly, and maybe from afar.

So be yourself. Even when it feels easier to blend in, stay connected to what makes you different. Your experiences, your way of seeing things, they're not flaws. They're your signature.

When you're honest with yourself, you understand what helps you grow, what holds you back, and what you truly need. You stop bending to fit into someone else's frame and start standing in your own.

When you stay true to yourself, you build better boundaries, stronger relationships, and a deeper trust in your own voice. Self-acceptance becomes your anchor. You move through life with more clarity and less comparison.

Let authenticity lead. In a world constantly trying to shape you, have the courage to shape yourself. The most Nobel things one can give to yourself—**is simply *you*.**

"If you cannot see the beauty in yourself, who will see the beauty within you?"

Honour Your Values to attain Inner Peace

To live a fulfilling life, one that feels honest and whole, you have to stay true to who you are. Don't trade your truth for approval. The world is full of voices telling you who to be, what to want, how to live. But you're not here to echo those voices; you're here to listen to your own. You don't need to chase popular opinions or measure yourself against the expectations of society, family, or friends especially when those standards don't sit well with your soul.

Authenticity isn't always easy. Sometimes, being true to yourself means standing alone or walking a different path. But that path is yours and it's sacred. Trust what feels real and right to you, even when it's uncomfortable. Respect your own feelings as you would a dear friend's. Be honest with yourself about what truly brings you peace, meaning, and joy.

"When you chase what's not meant for you, you're differing from what is meant for you." In trying to fit into molds that weren't made for you, you might miss the very things that would light you up from within.

So live gently, but firmly, in alignment with your values. **Please yourself not in selfishness, but in sincerity.** The joy that comes from that kind of living isn't loud, but it's lasting. Nobody knows you better than you. Spend time with yourself. Get curious. Ask questions. Explore your strengths, your wounds, your hopes. In that self-awareness lies your compass.

Stay true. That's where your power is. That's where your purpose lives.

Note: *Living a life that is true to yourself does not necessarily mean ignoring the opinions or feelings of others, but rather it means being true to your values and beliefs whilst still showing empathy and respect towards others.*

By balancing your own needs and desires with the needs and feelings of those around you, you can maintain healthy relationships while still living a life that is true to yourself. You cannot do whatever you want without considering the ramifications and consequences of your actions.

You need to ensure that your actions align with your values and beliefs and take responsibility for your reactions to any challenges or obstacles that may arise. Besides that, you need to be accountable for your actions and decisions, as well as the consequences that follow.

Develop a sense of self-understanding.

Nobody wants to wake up hoping for problems in their life, yet life's unpredictability places trials along our path — financial burdens, heartbreaks that leave us breathless, health scares that shake our confidence, career detours that challenge our sense of direction. These storms arrive uninvited, often when we feel least prepared to face them. But to weather them with grace, we must do more than endure; we must understand ourselves, not just on the surface, but at the core of who we are.

Without that inner clarity, we lose our sense of direction — decisions feel heavier, emotions unpredictable, and even simple moments become tangled in uncertainty. Life begins to feel like crossing a crowded street blindfolded, uncertain, reactive, and risky. Imagine a blind person attempting to move through a busy intersection without guidance. It's not a matter of willpower, but of awareness. Likewise, walking through life without knowing yourself, your patterns, your triggers, your wounds and wisdom is no less disorienting.

To move through difficulty, we must learn to listen inward: to observe our thoughts without judgment, to understand the emotions that rise like waves, and to gently trace them back to the currents beneath. When we don't, we fall into reflexes that harm more than help. But when we do, when we begin to see ourselves clearly, we no longer stumble through confusion. We begin to respond, not react. We begin to choose with intention. Clarity takes root, and from it grows resilience.

There was a time when I chased the fleeting pleasures of parties and nights spent without consequence or so I thought. I lived for the moment, dismissing the cost. Money slipped through my fingers. Whenever I stumbled, I leaned on my parents for support, unaware that I was repeating a cycle that only postponed the reckoning. Eventually, the support dried up, and I was left alone with the reality of my choices. It was sobering not just financially, but emotionally. That's when I began to see: **joy is not the same as fulfilment. Fun, without direction, can turn into escape**.

There is nothing wrong with joy. In fact, it is essential. But without balance, without self-awareness, joy loses its depth. It becomes noise instead of music. What grounds us is the ability to choose not only what feels good in the moment, but what honors who we want to become. The most centered people I've met—those who seem deeply rooted in both calm and clarity share a common trait: they know themselves. They don't act from impulse alone. They pause, they reflect, and they align their actions with values that are not easily shaken by passing emotions or outside approval.

And so I say: give yourself the time to meet yourself. Reflect on your experiences not to judge them, but to learn. Trace your feelings back to their origin. Ask yourself why you choose what you choose. The more intimately you know yourself, the easier it becomes to make choices that nourish your life instead of complicating it.

When you understand yourself, the world's noise softens. You no longer bend under the pressure to fit in, to please, to perform. You learn to say no when something doesn't sit right and to say yes only when your heart aligns. Approval becomes another bonus, not a desperate need. You begin to build a life that feels real, not rehearsed. One where peace is no longer something you chase but something that rises from within.

Learn to enjoy your own company. Be at ease in your own presence. That is where true belonging begins. You are not here to be anyone else. Your dreams, your strengths, your truths they are yours alone. Don't diminish them by comparison. Instead, cherish them. Water them.

Ask yourself:
What do I truly care about?
What makes me come alive?
Who do I wish to become?

Answering these questions isn't the end, it's the beginning. A beginning that leads you not away from the world, but home to yourself. And once you are at home within, the world around you begins to shift, too. Not because it changes, but because you have.

> *When we aim to align our actions with our desires, we must first look inward deeply and honestly. This requires curiosity, not just about ourselves, but about the world around us. A willingness to learn, explore new ideas, and embrace different perspectives expands our understanding and shapes our growth.*
>
> *Life experience becomes our greatest teacher when we choose to see every moment, every challenge, and every joy as an opportunity to evolve. Through consistent self-reflection and intentional self-discovery, we move closer to our fullest potential.*
>
> *And as this awareness deepens, something beautiful begins to unfold: a strong sense of purpose, meaning, and fulfilment. This is the essence of self-actualization—the subtle confidence of becoming who we were always meant to be.*

<u>Be honest with yourself.</u>

We spend years becoming who the world wants us to be and then spend a lifetime aching to return to who we truly are. To live a life that feels whole, one must begin with a kind of courage—the courage to meet oneself, not the version crafted for the world, but the one that waits beneath the surface, raw and unguarded. Understanding who you truly are begins with an act of radical honesty. This honesty is not gentle; it asks you to stand before the mirror without flinching, to recognize your strengths without arrogance, your flaws without shame, and your limitations without fear. It requires you to confront your discomfort, to acknowledge the truths that don't fit neatly into expectations—those may be messy, inconvenient, or even painful. But only when you stop running from them can you begin to live in alignment with who you are, not who you've been pretending to be.

You cannot live a full life if your soul is only half seen. Imagine working in a job that feels foreign to your values, suffocating in a culture that drains you, yet staying for the pay check, the friendships, or the comfort of routine. You begin to silence your truth, justifying the dissonance with phrases like, *"It's not that bad,"* or *"It's only temporary."* But beneath that surface calm, something inside you begins to fray. Can you truly thrive in a space where your inner voice is silenced? What begins as a compromise slowly becomes self-abandonment. You might not notice it at first, but over time, it clouds your clarity, disturbs your emotional balance, and holds back the personal growth your soul quietly longs for.

When you ignore your deeper feelings and suppress your authentic thoughts, you don't protect your peace you postpone your evolution. Growth does not come through denial, but through acceptance. And clarity—the kind that simplifies life and strips it of pretence only arrives when you start being honest with yourself. That is the ground on which authenticity is built. It's not just the beginning of self-discovery; it's the very soil from which all meaningful relationships must grow, including the one you hold with your own.

Consider a relationship where you silence your dissatisfaction, support your partner unconditionally even when it depletes you, and hide your true needs behind smiles and silence. You let them drift into pleasures that exclude you, you give when you're already in debt, and all the while you pretend it's okay. Is that love or the slow erosion of self-worth? When we avoid honest conversations with our partners, cracks begin to form in the foundation of trust. But when we avoid honesty with ourselves, we begin to lose touch with who we are. In both cases, the result is the same: disconnection, resentment, and an ache for something more genuine.

To live fully is to live truthfully. The path to personal growth begins when you stop hiding. Be unapologetically real with yourself. Embrace your uniqueness, your contradictions, and your burning questions. Let your core values and not your fears shape your choices. And when you do, the world no longer feels like a stage, but like a home. You will walk lighter, live clearer, and love deeper. For in the quiet act of self-honesty, you unlock the freedom to live a life that is not only full, but fully yours.

Growth does not wait for perfect conditions. It begins the moment we choose action over complaint, effort over excuses, and courage over comfort. What you shape today becomes the path you walk tomorrow.

Where Complaints End, Wisdom Begins:

The weak curse the wind, blame the waves, and drown in 'if only.' But the strong? They waste no breath on storms they cannot command, they adjust their sails with wisdom. While others wait for mercy from the sea, the brave find motion even in chaos.

I've accomplished nothing worthwhile by sitting still and reciting my sorrows. Complaining may offer a moment's of comfort, but it builds nothing. I've never seen anyone rise to greatness by pointing fingers or drowning in self-pity. The ones who inspire, the ones whose lives stir something deep within us share one common truth: they take ownership of their lives without fear, without excuses.

They do not spend their days dwelling on what went wrong. They rise, even when the weight of the world leans hard against them. They rise from the dim corners of difficulty and lean into the light even if it's faint, trusting that even a glimmer can guide the next step forward.

Success, as I've seen it, doesn't come from perfect conditions. It comes from imperfect people choosing not to remain still. It comes from those who don't sit and curse the rain, but learn to plant seeds right in the heart of the storm and turning hardship into harvest.

Consider Lady Gaga, an artist whose rise shines through courage and creative defiance. Born Stefani Germanotta, she faced rejection and skepticism but never let the noise drown her voice. Instead of letting setbacks hold her back, she used them as fuel to transform pain into powerful anthems that resonate worldwide. Her journey is not just about fame, it's about owning her truth, breaking barriers, and crafting a legacy from vulnerability and strength.

Or Sundar Pichai, who grew up in a home with modest means but never let those walls define the size of his dreams. He didn't blame his circumstances; he studied them, rose through them, and grew beyond them.

Then there's Mark Zuckerberg, who began in a college dorm, facing doubt and criticism, but kept creating. He didn't spend his days explaining why things were hard. He kept building, changing how the world connects.

These people have one thing in common: they channel their energy into solutions, **not sorrow**. They reshape their reality not by wishing it changed, but by changing it through action. Where others see dead ends, they carve new paths. Where others halt at resistance, they press forward with relentless will.

If this truth hasn't yet taken root in you, try this: choose someone who moves you; not as a distant idol, but as a teacher. Study them. Not with envy, but with the focus of an artist studying a masterpiece, dissecting the strokes that built it.

Ask yourself:

- *How did they face setbacks and still move forward?*
- *How did they remain steady when the world turned uncertain?*
- *How did they hold on to vision when the road got rough?*
- *How did they accept their flaws and keep refining themselves?*

Don't just ask, but absorb. Reflect. Learn until their grit becomes the mirror in which you recognize your own strength.

The truth is simple: growth belongs to those who act, not those who wait. They don't beg for calm skies; they learn to dance in the storm. They understand that life owes no one comfort—only the raw materials of a canvas. What they paint is theirs alone to decide, stroke by deliberate stroke. And your own masterpiece? It's still unfolding. This is your moment to stop narrating your pain and start shaping your path. Let the fire shape you, not burn you.

A success story from my high school friend:

While speaking of resilience, I'm reminded of a friend from high school; someone who once struggled with studies but now serves as an officer in the Delhi Police. He wasn't known for academic brilliance then. In fact, many thought he would never make it. But he never allowed that judgment to define him. He didn't complain. He simply began.

What set him apart wasn't natural intelligence, it was perseverance. He knew where he stood and what he lacked, but instead of hiding behind excuses, he leaned into the challenge. He stayed after class to seek help, asked questions others were too proud to ask, and immersed himself in every space where learning lived—be it school workshops, debates, or competitions. Wherever knowledge was offered, he showed up, hungry and humble.

His path wasn't smooth. He failed, often. He was mocked, ridiculed, even belittled by classmates and ignored by those who measured worth only in marks. Some girls in the class would sneer, and boys would bully. Others laughed at his failures, treating them like a sport. Yet through it all, he never folded into bitterness. He never played the victim.

He understood early on that complaints don't pave the road to growth, but effort does. Every setback became a lesson, every failure a forge. He turned his academic misfortunes into stepping stones. Today, he stands with pride in a uniform he earned not through brilliance, but through relentless will.

In contrast, I remember others, those naturally gifted students who topped every exam without breaking a sweat. Teachers praised them, classmates gravitated toward them, and their names were often held up as the gold standard of success. Yet, when faced with the slightest inconvenience, they were quick to complain, expecting exceptions. They leaned heavily on their intelligence, but rarely stepped beyond the classroom to challenge themselves.

Despite their early shine, I don't recall any remarkable feats from them outside academics. They were smart, *yes*, but confined within the walls of their own comfort.

Academic success is important, that without a question. It lays the foundation. But a foundation is only the beginning. Pride in one's grades, without the hunger to grow beyond them, becomes a ceiling rather than a launchpad. True growth demands a willingness to fail, to be humbled, and to rise stronger.

What matters more than scores is the spirit to learn. A growth mindset is a steady belief that you can improve, one that turns obstacles into invitations and mistakes into learning. It teaches us to face challenges and treat effort as a bridge rather than a burden. Such a mindset not only sharpens the mind, it shapes the spirit.

When you believe that your abilities can evolve with effort, you open yourself to a life of endless discovery. Challenges no longer intimidate—they instruct. Mistakes are no longer signs of weakness, they are steps toward strength.

So let us stop complaining about the weight we must carry. Let us instead see it as a tool for our becoming. As Albert Einstein once said, *"Once you stop learning, you start dying."* The moment we stop believing in our potential to grow, we confine ourselves to who we were, not who we could become.

Adopt the mindset that every difficulty is a lesson in disguise, every failure a disguised teacher. In doing so, we don't just pass exams, we learn how to live.

<u>Religion perspective:</u>

According too many regions teaching: You already have what you need. Life isn't working against you; it's guiding you, even when it doesn't feel that way. Things don't just happen randomly; there's a purpose behind them, even if you can't see it yet. So instead of resisting where you are, try to trust that there's a reason for it.

Every experience, good or bad, helps you grow. The hard times aren't punishments. They're lessons, shaping you into the person you're meant to become. The obstacles you face? They're not stopping you; they're showing you the way forward.

When life feels difficult, it's not because you're failing. It's because you're being prepared. You're not crumbling—you're changing. Slowly, steadily, you're becoming stronger, wiser, and more compassionate through what you go through.

So don't run from the tough moments. They're like rain; uncomfortable, but necessary for growth. Every struggle has something to teach you. What feels like a setback might actually be steering you toward something better. What feels like waiting might be giving you time to get ready for what's next.

When life feels heavy, remember: You're not falling apart. You're being rearranged, piece by piece, into the person you're meant to be. So, trust where you are. Trust the timing. And most importantly, trust yourself. When you stop fighting the present moment, you start building the life that's truly yours.

*That day, my mom was unable to help me and unable to find excuses for me. She was sitting beside me, watching quietly with disappointment on her face. With a hint of sadness and concern, she said, **"I failed you; you took advantage of my love."** Hearing that, I had no words to respond to her emotional revelation, so my tears felt pity for me, saying sorry through my cheeks.*

I was deeply hurt that day, not because I failed the selection exam or because my dad scolded me, but because I realized that I had betrayed the trust and love that my parents had for me. I know I failed the selection exam, but most importantly, I realize I failed my parents.

The voices of my mom and dad are still echoing in my mind, reminding me every time I feel like complaining or making excuses for my own mistakes.

*One of my dad's lectures on that day is still trapped in my mind, He said, **"Only the weak people who don't have much knowledge or strength to face their own challenges like a real man will complain and make excuses like a weak baby, hoping that their parents might be able to fix everything for them, but in the long run they only end up hindering their own growth and development.***

He told me that if you can't be the hero of your life, then you will always be stuck in a cycle of dependency and never be able to reach your full potential. As a result, your life will not be different from that of a street bagger struggling to survive on the streets. Taking excuses and begging others for a penny to fill their empty stomachs. and it is up to you to choose whether you want to continue making excuses and relying on others, or you want to take responsibility for your actions and become the hero of your own life

<u>Note:</u> *I'm sharing my personal experience with you because I love you and I want you to be the hero of your life and not the victim of your immature mindset.*

Peace is not born from reshaping the world to suit our desires, nor from waiting for life to become easier or fairer. It grows within us when we learn to master the way we see what unfolds before us. The world will always move in its own rhythm, offering both beauty and challenge, clarity and confusion. When our vision is ruled by fear, comparison, or resistance, even calm moments feel heavy. Yet when we train our perception with patience, understanding, and acceptance, the same world begins to feel lighter. Peace, then, is not a reward granted by circumstances. It appears when our eyes learn to rest on reality without demanding it to be different.

Master your mind.

The power to find what you seek lies in how you choose to see.

If you're reading this book to find mistakes, I promise—you'll find them. But if you're here to grow, to reflect, and to learn, you'll gain something meaningful. That's the beauty of how we see the world: we find what we look for. And that's what I want this book to be for you: a mirror that reflects not just the words I've written, but the lens through which you choose to read them.

Over the years, I've spoken with many people, listened to their stories, and studied what drives us. And one thing is clear; we hold within us an inner power. **The power to become who we dream of becoming**, the power to build a life we truly want. But in that same space, we also carry the ability to limit ourselves. To doubt. To judge too quickly. To let fear and bias shape our view.

What we believe, how we speak, and how we think all shape our reality. Our perception becomes the filter through which we see everything. We often see not the truth, but a reflection of our own assumptions. For example, imagine a man sitting on a bench, holding a cardboard sign that says, **"Homeless. Help me."** One person might think he's lazy.

Another might believe he's a drug addict. Someone else might feel pity and offer help. But the truth? No one really knows his story.

Maybe he lost everything in an economic downturn. Maybe he was robbed far from home. Or maybe he simply needs someone to see him with compassion instead of judgment. Before we rush to conclusions, it's worth asking, what does our reaction reveal? Often, our reactions say more about us than they do about him.

The point is, *our minds make quick judgments based on limited information and often, those judgments reflect our internal beliefs more than external reality.* We don't always care about what's real; we care about confirming what we already believe.

Some believe God is real. Others believe He is not. Perhaps God exists. Perhaps not. But maybe the deeper truth isn't found in proving or disproving, it lives in what we choose to believe. Our perception becomes the canvas on which we paint our reality. It's not always about what is, but about what we are willing or unwilling to see.

If we've decided to see the world through a negative lens, we'll keep finding reasons to justify it. But if we choose to see with openness and understanding, we might discover a completely different world, one filled with empathy, growth, and unexpected connection.

Positive thinking paves the way to a fulfilling life.

We have the power to either limit ourselves or expand our perspectives; the power to narrow our vision or open ourselves to deeper understanding. Each day, in ways both small and big, we are choosing what to focus on, what to absorb, what to give life to in our minds. And in those choices, we are slowly shaping the world we experience.

If we look for darkness, we will surely find it. But if we look for light, even in dim corners, we will find that too. The world, in many ways, becomes a mirror, reflecting not just what is, but what we're willing to see. Our beliefs, our expectations, our attitude, all these become the lens through which reality forms.

When you believe you are unworthy, your mind begins to gather proof. And when you believe you are enough as you are, imperfect but growing you begin to see reasons to trust that truth. In this way, belief is not just a thought; it is the director of your experience.

Let's say there's a person in your life; a friend, perhaps, who often frustrates you. Their words sting, their presence unsettles you. It's easy to fall into the habit of judgment: *"He's awful... just a terrible person."* You share your frustrations with others, perhaps hoping to find release. And yet, pause for a moment then ask who is carrying the heavier weight? Whose mind is filling with unease?

If someone crosses a boundary or treats you poorly, you always have a choice. You can speak your truth or you can distance yourself quietly from the scene. But blaming, labeling, or gossiping does little more than multiply the hurt within you, and around you. When you paint someone as the villain, you unwittingly cast yourself as the victim. And that role, though it might feel justified, it rarely leads to peace.

Maybe they were unkind. But does passing that pain forward make the world softer or harsher? At some point, you must decide: will I be a mirror of pain, or a wellspring of healing?

"The peace you seek does not come from changing others, but from choosing how you see them."

Choosing a positive path doesn't mean ignoring what's wrong. It means meeting difficulty with awareness, not bitterness. It means honoring your feelings without feeding your resentment. You can set boundaries and still hold compassion. You can walk away and still wish them well. That is strength.

And yes, you do have that strength. You have the power to change not just your thoughts, but the tone of your life. You can soften the noise in your mind, or fill it with light. Every moment is a chance to choose again.

You are not at the mercy of your thoughts. You are their author. You are not a prisoner of your past. You are the Master of your next step. Be mindful of the thoughts you nurture. Be tender with the beliefs you carry. They are the soil from which your life grows. Use your power with care,

Choose wisely. And always choose in the direction of peace.

<u>**Emotional control is the foundation of healthy relationships.**</u>

To see another as an enemy is not strength, it is the mind's silent surrender. True mastery begins not with domination over others, but with sovereignty over one's own thoughts. It is the art of meeting chaos with clarity, pain with understanding, and conflict with an unshaken calm.

People who master their minds don't just react to life, they shape it from within. When storms arise, they are the steady flame that bends but does not extinguish. They know that every setback is a hidden lesson, every obstacle a chance to refine their spirit. And in this way, life becomes not a battle to be won, but a terrain that reveals its meaning only to those who move through it with attention.

Study the people around you not to judge, but to understand. *How they speak, how they behave and what is the reason behind; there's always a back story.* The disciplined mind observes without condemnation, engages without hostility, and responds without bitterness. It does not confuse boundaries with walls, nor justice with vengeance.

And yet, this mastery is not cold detachment. It is the courage to feel deeply while choosing wisely. To say, *"This pain will not define me."* To whisper, *"I will not pass this hurt along."* To decide, moment by moment, that though the world may be harsh, you need not add to its sharp edges, you can be the place where the hurting stops and the healing begins.

You hold a power far greater than you may realize: the power to choose. You can guide your thoughts, steady your emotions, and meet life as someone who takes ownership of the inner world, not as a prisoner of habit. Every decision, small yet strong in its influence, shapes the direction of your life.

So when the weight of the world presses in, remember: the mind is not a cage, but a canvas. You are not here to play a game, but to compose a life. And every thought you nurture, every belief you cradle, is a brushstroke upon that canvas. Choose them with care. Choose them with kindness. And above all, choose them in the direction of peace.

Your growth does not begin when you feel strong, prepared, or complete. It begins the moment you are willing to face your weakness with honesty, without disguise or denial. What you call a flaw is often only a place still learning how to stand. Within every hesitation, every unfinished part, something is quietly forming. There is beauty not only in who you are becoming, but in every part of you still in the process of rising.

The beauty of weakness

The moments when you feel shattered often carry within them the seeds of the strongest parts of yourself.

No two people are the same. Each of us carries a constellation of strengths and weaknesses that make us entirely unique. It is this contrast within and among us that gives depth and meaning to the human experience. If life were stripped of struggle and imperfection, if everything unfolded in perfect symmetry and ease, would growth still have meaning? Would learning hold value? Would fulfillment even be possible?

Imagine a world where everyone is flawless, every path smooth, every task mastered at birth. Without hardship, there would be no striving. *Without gaps, no reaching. And without reaching, no becoming.* In such a world, life would not flourish, it would stagnate. The essence of being human would be lost in the uniformity of perfection. Weakness, then, is not a flaw to be eradicated, but a thread in the fabric of our evolution. It shows us where we can grow, where we can stretch beyond the known, and where we can rise.

Think of a traffic signal. If all we ever saw was green signal, would the roads truly be safer? Without red or yellow lights to guide and regulate flow, chaos would ensue. Accidents would become inevitable. The very system that allows movement would collapse under the weight of its imbalance. In the same way, if our lives were all green lights; endless momentum without pause or resistance, balance would disappear. The moments of hesitation, uncertainty, and challenge are not interruptions to life's rhythm; they are part of its design. They guide us, humble us, and call forth the deeper parts of who we are.

To grow, we must first see. And to see clearly, we must be willing to look honestly at the places within us that feel unsure or incomplete. Avoiding weakness builds walls around potential. When we turn toward our fragility with curiosity rather than shame, it becomes a mirror reflecting our capacity to change.

Consider the simple desire to ride a bicycle. At first, you lack balance, coordination, confidence. You might fall, hesitate, even fear the motion itself. But if the longing to ride outweighs the fear of falling, you begin. And in beginning, you grow. The act of trying however clumsy becomes the path to freedom. That is the true beauty of weakness: it reveals not just what we lack, but what we're willing to reach for.

Avoiding weakness may feel safe, but it comes at a cost. A fear of public speaking, for example, will not vanish through avoidance. Confidence is not gifted by time; it is grown through courage. When we face the fear, speak the trembling words, stand in our vulnerability, something shifts. Not all at once. But over time, fear transforms into strength. Hesitation becomes presence. And what once seemed impossible begins to feel natural.

Growth does not arrive fully formed. It stumbles in, wearing the clothes of discomfort and doubt. But every stumble carries its own promise. It asks for patience. It asks for effort. And it asks for a willingness to believe that we are more than our limitations. The path is not without setbacks, but the journey continues, if only we choose to step forward.

To recognize our weakness is not to admit defeat. It is to begin the work for becoming. In meeting ourlimits with compassion, we open the door to transformation. And with each step, we remember: the parts of us that seem most fragile may be the very parts that carry the seeds of our greatest strength.

"If life had no cracks, light would never find a way in" -
Leonard Cohen's

<u>**Weakness is a sign of growth.**</u>

You do not need to hide your flaws or mask your weaknesses in order to appear strong. Strength does not bloom from the illusion of perfection, but from the courage to face what is imperfect within us. Weakness, when understood rightly, is not a defect, it is an invitation. It emerges as part of the learning process and gently points us toward the areas where growth is most needed.

To know our weakness is to map the terrain of our becoming. It is the beginning of self-awareness and the root of transformation. When we acknowledge the parts of ourselves that feel unfinished, we create space for intention, for effort, and ultimately, for change. Through deliberate practice and patient engagement, what once felt like a limitation becomes a bridge to competence and confidence.

Imagine a person who chooses passivity over responsibility, expecting others to carry their burdens and solve their problems. Without the willingness to recognize and respond to their own weaknesses, can they truly grow? Can they develop the inner strength or wisdom needed to move through life with purpose? It would be no different than placing an untrained driver behind the controls of a spacecraft; no direction, no grounding, no mastery.

But when a person dares to be vulnerable; when they meet their shortcomings with honesty and resolve, they set themselves on a path of genuine transformation. There is strength in that humility. There is beauty in that effort. To admit we do not yet know is the first act of true learning. It is not weakness that holds us back, but the refusal to engage with it.

A baby does not fear the fall when learning to walk. They do not compare themselves to others or question whether they are flawed. They simply try falling, rising, and trying again. Their focus is not on perfection but on progress. Each stumble is part of the story. Each small step a celebration of becoming. They do not conceal their limits; they outgrow them with time, patience, and trust.

In much the same way, we must remember that our own weaknesses are not to be shamed or silenced, but understood. They reveal the edges of our potential, the places where we have yet to bloom. Growth does not come from pretending to be whole, but from the grace of being unfinished and willing.

When we embrace this, we begin to see that our imperfections are not obstacles to growth; they are part of the journey itself. They guide us toward becoming more capable, more compassionate, and more complete. Weakness, then, is not a failure to be fixed but a teacher to be welcomed.

"We spend so long hiding what is imperfect, not realizing that our imperfections are the language through which life teaches us to evolve".

We live in a world that often mistakes performance for strength and silence for composure. Strength is paraded as the absence of struggle—flawless, efficient, invulnerable. We applaud the image of those who never falter, never weep, never need. But this is not strength. This is a carefully crafted illusion.

Society glorifies a version of perfection so rigid that it leaves no room for error, no space for the messy truth of becoming. Mistakes are viewed not as part of the learning curve, but as stains on one's worth. And in a culture that worships image over authenticity, people begin to hide; afraid that one misstep will define them, erase them, and disqualify them.

This false narrative has consequences. It silences the very voices that long to speak, paralyzes those who wish to rise, and dims the light of countless dreams before they are even given a chance. Many do not pursue what calls them, not due to a lack of desire or potential, but out of fear. Fear of not being enough. Fear of being judged. Fear of failing in a world that pretends perfection is real and failure is shameful.

But strength does not come from pretending. True strength lies in the courage to be seen as you are where you are. It lives in the willingness to try, to falter, and to begin again. There is more bravery in honest vulnerability than in polished performance.

Let us not chase the shadow of strength society offers— polished, hollow, untouchable. Let us instead honor the true power of those who dare to be real. Those who fall and rise, not to impress, but to evolve. For there is nothing more human, more honest, or more beautiful than that.

Note: Weaknesses reveal opportunities for growth that perfection would otherwise obscure.

What appears as loss is not always an ending. Often, it is life rearranging itself to make space for who we are becoming. The moments that confuse you, the questions that stay unanswered, the pain that refuses to leave; all carry something hidden. They are not empty experiences. Each one holds a lesson you could not have learned any other way. What once felt like absence reveals itself as guidance, shaping us in ways we could not yet understand.

The lesson I have learned.

The pain and confusion I once resisted slowly turned into a path of their own. They pulled me inward toward clarity, then outward toward growth.

People often say $2 + 2 = 4$. It's simple, straight forward. But for me, life has never followed the straight line. My life looks more like $(2 - 2) + (2 + 2) = 4$. I've had to lose before I could gain. I've had to empty before I could be filled. My story hasn't moved in straight lines like others, and perhaps that's what makes it mine.

I've known adversity intimately. I've cried into pillows that held more of my soul than any conversation ever could. Night after night, sleep slipped through my fingers as I wrestled with an ache I couldn't name; feeling lost, suspended in the still chaos of unanswered questions. There were evenings I sat quietly at my study table, and without warning, tears would gather like rain clouds in my eyes, spilling down my cheeks as I tried to keep my pain invisible.

Sometimes, I found myself on the rooftop under the silent company of the moon, counting stars not because I believed I could, but because I hoped that somewhere between the silence and the sky, I might stumble upon a reason, an answer, or at least a little peace.

And then came the questions; those relentless, echoing *whys*:

- Why do I face so many trials when I've done nothing wrong, but try to be good?
- Why does pain visit me when all I long for is peace?
- Why does my kindness seem to invite rejection, and my loyalty lead to betrayal?
- Why does my love feel invisible, my efforts misunderstood?

I kept asking, again and again, as if repetition might summon an answer. But the only reply was silence and a growing emptiness that no amount of reasoning could soothe. I searched tirelessly for meaning, hoping that one day, this entire inner struggle would lead to something better... for me, and for those I care about.

I hoped, perhaps naively, that they would see my heart. That they would understand the depth of what I gave. But too often, I felt like I was speaking into an abyss like someone trying to start a fire in the middle of a storm. And I wondered: Does this make me foolish? Is love a weakness? Is kindness misplaced?

But no; I refuse to believe that love is foolishness. I refuse to equate care with naiveté. These are not weaknesses. These are strengths misunderstood by those not ready to receive them. We were raised to believe that love, compassion, and kindness are virtues to uphold. Our faiths and cultures all echo the same truth: *love is the greatest of all.*

So why, then, does it hurt so much to love?

- If love leads to rejection, then what is love?
- If care is unappreciated, then what is care?
- If kindness is overlooked, then what is kindness?

Why teach these values if the world doesn't seem to recognize them? Why give so much of our hearts if what we receive is silence or worse, scorn?

And so, the conclusion I came to is this:

- *Love is not wrong, but it becomes weary when it is not seen.*
- *Care is not wasted, but it longs to be met with gratitude.*
- *Kindness is not naive, but it needs a space where it is understood.*

Giving endlessly to those who cannot recognize your heart is like pouring water into a bucket full of holes. It's like singing beautiful songs to a room full of deaf people, no matter how pure the melody, it reaches no ears, touches no soul. And while love asks us to give unconditionally, wisdom asks us to give wisely.

A healthy relationship—any meaningful connection requires more than one heart giving. Like a car cannot run on one wheel, love cannot move forward when only one person is carrying it. Love thrives when both hearts lean in, when care is met with gratitude and kindness with understanding, when giving is met with receiving, and when effort is mirrored in intention.

It's not about giving 50% and waiting for the rest. It's about both souls showing up fully 100% to 100%, heart to heart. That is where healing begins, where love grows roots.

So, if you've been asking yourself these same questions; if you've felt unheard, unseen, unappreciated, know this: your love is not meaningless. Your kindness is not in vain. But perhaps it's time to protect your heart with the same grace you offer others. Offer your light where it is welcomed. Speak your truth where it can be heard. Even the sun, as generous as it is, does not shine forever on a single place. It moves. And so must we.

Love grows better once the heart releases what no longer serves it. An ending often shifts into a fresh start with more wisdom.

__What I do now:__

I've come to see slowly and through experience, that love is not a rule, but a subtle truth: we are not meant to become cold, harsh, or unkind. Love should never lose its warmth. But we must learn to invest in relationships where love is *recognized*, and where care is *appreciated*. Even the deepest devotion has its limits and rightly so. We should never offer ourselves blindly, without asking whether our love is seen, valued, or returned in kind.

Everything in love must be rooted in **mutual recognition**. Without it, even the most sincere efforts can lead to imbalance, resentment, and emotional emptiness.

You see, loving someone doesn't mean they owe us the same in return. I may love someone deeply, yet if they do not feel the same, I must honor their truth. Love, in its highest form, does not cross another's boundaries. It does not demand, or force. And this applies to all relationships, romantic, platonic, or familial.

One of the truest sayings is, *"If you love someone, set them free."* And here's what that really means:

- If your absence brings them peace, then let them have it.
- If your presence feels heavy to them, then walk away from them.
- If their joy blooms only when you are gone, then let them pursue that joy, without guilt or resistance.

That is what love looks like when it grows beyond the ego.

To truly love is to let them be free—to smile on their own terms, to choose their own path, to become fully themselves without bending to our hopes or needs. Love is not possession. Love is not control. Love is not shaping someone into what we want them to be.

And yes, don't you want to see them smile? Don't you want to see them truly happy, even if that happiness isn't shaped by you?

Let love be a space where two souls can breathe; where both are free to grow, to stumble, to heal, and to become. Let it be a union of kindness and clarity, not a prison of unspoken demands.

Even if you believe you know what's best for them, let them choose. Wisdom lies in letting go of control. True care is courageous enough to trust someone's journey, even when it doesn't include you.

But while you give love freely, **never give away your self-respect**.

- Offer your freedom, but don't surrender it.
- Share your love, but don't let it be used against you.
- Give your kindness, but not at the cost of your well-being.
- Care deeply, but not to the point of self-erasure.

Love should never require you to abandon yourself. Respect the other, but never forget to respect your own voice, your own needs, your own spirit.

This is how we create meaningful, healthy connections—by giving fully, without losing ourselves. By being kind without being exploited. By supporting without being diminished.

In simple terms: **Love freely. Support gently. And never confuse surrender with self-sacrifice.** Let love be a bridge, not a burden. Let it uplift you both.

Many become the victims of their own love and kindness not because they are weak, but because their hearts were never taught to stop giving. They pour themselves into others, hoping sincerity will be enough, that love will heal all wounds. But too often, they are left standing in the rain of their own expectations, holding the weight of unspoken pain.

Yet rain, when endured too long, erodes even the strongest stones. Among them, a few—just a few—begin to understand: love is not meant to come at the cost of themselves. They gather the scattered pieces of their being and begin the subtle journey of standing up, not in anger, but in understanding.

And in that standing? A revelation. They learn to walk away from doors that no longer open with love. Lonely as it may first feel, this is not an end, but a homecoming. With each step, they reclaim something sacred: their peace, their voice, the worth they once mortgaged for acceptance. They discover, at last, that love in its truest form does not ask them to shrink. It asks them to rise.

Every habit starts as a shelter, a space where life feels lighter. Stay too long, the shelter turns into a cage. Living well comes from sensing the right moment to stay or step away.

The Quiet Art of Habits

Every habit carries a hidden story whether it's to ease discomfort, cut the noise of life, or simply help us get by. Often, they begin as small acts of self-preservation, a way to soothe the ache or offer something familiar in a world that feels uncertain and shifting. But what begins as comfort can, in time, become something else entirely, a weight we carry without knowing why.

I remember December 2020, the heart of the COVID pandemic. My friend and I were confined to a modest apartment in Delhi; just two beds, a small hall, attached to a small kitchen, and a single window that looked out onto an empty street. The city had gone silent, as if the world stopped breathing. Time moved slowly. Days bled into nights, and the future felt like a question no one could answer.

It started one cold evening. We lit our first cigarette not out of craving, but out of stillness. Something to do with our hands. Something warm to draw into our lungs whiles the world outside felt frozen. The first few were shared between us—two or three a day, no more. We laughed at how it made us cough, and at how strange it felt to enjoy something we had once sworn off. But slowly, there's a changed. The cigarettes became part of the silence, part of the routine. A pack found its way into the drawer. Then another. Mornings began with smoke curling toward the ceiling. Evenings ended with ash on the windowsill. What had felt like relief began to feel like need.

At first, it felt harmless; almost tender, how easily it wove itself into our days. But habits don't always announce their arrival. They slip in unnoticed, wearing the face of comfort.

No one sets out to form a habit that takes from them. Often, it begins with a simple intention: to cope. To get through. But some habits stay longer than we planned. They sink into the corners of our lives and call themselves necessary, even as they slowly erode what we never meant to lose.

I'm not here to judge those who lean on something when the world grows too heavy. I know that ache; the kind that sits in your chest, silent but constant, urging you to reach for anything that softens the pain. I've been there myself. Sometimes, we do what we must just to feel okay, just to keep the darkness at bay.

But there's a difference between surviving and healing. Survival keeps us breathing; healing invites us to live fully, openly, without hiding from the parts of ourselves that need care.

And the heart of the matter is this: we create habits to hold us, to serve us but sometimes, they begin to hold us captive instead. When that happens, it's time to pause and ask ourselves, honestly: Is this habit helping me step closer to the person I want to be? Or is it pulling me further from who I am meant to become?

If a habit no longer aligns with the future you desire, then the wisest choice is to let it go—early, and with intention, so you can reclaim your freedom to choose who you want to become.

Habits are the unseen hands that shape us persistently until, without noticing, we become their form.

Cultivate mindful habits

We are often on a journey of self-discovery and growth, facing moments of doubt, challenge, and confusion. Yet, these difficult times also bring opportunities for personal transformation. To walk this path with clarity and presence, cultivating mindful habits becomes essential.

Imagine coming home after a long, tiring day at work. You open the door and are immediately greeted by the warm scent of freshly baked cookies mingling with the rich aroma of coffee. Your mom smiles and says, *"My dear, I made your favorite cookies and brewed a fresh cup of coffee just for you. Go wash up; I've prepared warm water for your bath."* How would that moment stir your heart?

Most likely, a wave of calm and comfort washes over you, knowing someone has thoughtfully created a soothing space just for you.

It's not just the cookies or the coffee; it's the feeling of being seen, held, and gently cared for. In that moment, everything else fades. You feel safe. You breathe a little easier.

Imagine turning that same tenderness inward— creating moments that whisper, *you're safe, you're enough.* That is mindfulness at its core: not a practice of perfection, but a remembering. A remembering that presence itself can be a form of love.

When we begin to weave these mindful practices into our daily routines, we create a sanctuary of calm and positivity. This gentle awareness helps us manage stress, cultivate gratitude, and build a life that breathes with purpose and presence.

Early in my twenties, I struggled with self-doubt and the heavy weight of others' judgments. Questions about my worth and abilities clouded my mind and strained my relationships. I focused on my flaws and discomfort, missing out on life's possibilities. These doubts drained my energy and chipped away at my confidence.

Through the thick and thin of that journey, life itself became a teacher showing me, slowly but surely, that mindfulness is not some distant goal, but a gentle presence always available to meet me where I am. It taught me how to hold my fears and insecurities with kindness, to appreciate the present moment even when it's hard.

With mindfulness as my guide, I am learning to cultivate gratitude and self-compassion. Though I am still growing, this practice has softened the noise within me, gifting a quieter mind and a braver heart. I no longer rush to fix what feels broken; instead, I learn to sit with it, to listen. In that quiet acceptance, I've begun to taste something rare—a peace that doesn't depend on perfection, a freedom that grows from being at ease with myself.

<u>Building productive habits:</u>

Productive habits are quiet forces that shape our lives. Whether in our personal world or professional path, they help us move steadily toward the life we envision. They shape how we spend our days, and in time, how we define success, not in grand moments, but in the soft, steady rhythm of what we choose to repeat. When we cultivate the right habits, we create a rhythm that supports growth, clarity, and purpose—turning fleeting motivation into lasting momentum.

We often think of change as a leap. But most real change begins in a single decision, made in the stillness of an ordinary moment, to do something a little differently. To sit down and write one page. To wake up ten minutes earlier. To pause and breathe instead of react. Or to stop reaching for your phone first thing in the morning. These moments may seem small, but they speak volume to who we're becoming.

And yet, even as we reach for something new, we carry what no longer serves us. Change doesn't just ask us to begin, it also asks us to release. To create space, we must first become aware of what fills it. Often, it's not just time that's cluttered, but our patterns, our comforts, and the beliefs we've never questioned.

Yet before we build, we must first clear space. Some habits we've picked up without even noticing; through repetition, through comfort, or through fear. Some delay our growth; others quietly dim our clarity. Identifying and replacing them is not an act of punishment, but it's a quiet form of self-respect. It takes time. It takes tenderness. And it takes the willingness to fail and begin again, without shame.

When we understand the anatomy of a habit; the cue, the routine, the reward, it's like learning to read the language of our own behavior. For example: the scent of coffee might cue you to open your laptop. The ping of a notification might steer your focus away. These patterns, often invisible, quietly guide our choices. And when we begin to notice them, a kind of awakening happens, we start to see how much of our day is not decided by intention, but by repetition.

But awareness is only the first step. Insight must meet intention in a space that allows it to breathe. This is where environment enters; not just the physical, but the emotional. A cluttered space echoes in a cluttered mind. A word of encouragement can hold up a tired spirit. A phone within reach can undo an hour's worth of resolve. We thrive not by willpower alone, but by shaping spaces that gently support who we are trying to become.

In college, I used to cringe at how little effort I put into attending classes or improving my English. Back then, I was carefree, more drawn to laughter with friends than lecture halls. My English skills were poor, grammar shaky, vocabulary thin, and I often struggled to express my thoughts. It was frustrating. I began to notice how this limitation held me back, not just academically, but in my confidence and connection with others.

So I made my decision: Something had to change, but not everything at once. I began reading, just a few pages each night. I carried a small notebook, jotting down words that felt unfamiliar on my tongue. I listened to English podcasts, letting the cadence of fluent voices fill the silence of my room. I started to speak more. I stumbled often. Blushed more times than I can count. But I kept showing up. One small step, every single day.

Those simple practices became habits. And those habits became a bridge across my fears, into a language I once avoided. Reading didn't just improve my English. It widens my mind. It sharpened how I see the world. It even led me here, to this page, to this book (*one of the results of those habits is this book you're now reading.*). I don't call myself an expert, but I do know the power of a habit that grows from the inside out.

Still, what worked for me may not work for you. And that's the beauty of it. Habit-building is a personal alchemy. It requires experimentation, reflection, and the courage to begin again. There is no fixed formula—only questions: *What do I want more of in my life? What am I willing to do today? How can I make it just a little easier to choose the better path?*

Even when we find what works, it won't always come easily. Real change moves in quiet, uneven circles. Some days we show up with ease; other days, we slip. Progress is rarely loud; it looks like repetition, like returning to you after drifting away. The path isn't linear. There will be days you forget, days you resist. But the aim isn't perfection, its presence. It's the quiet decision to begin again, to keep choosing yourself in small, steady ways. That's how momentum builds; not in grand gestures, but in the soft weight of what we choose to repeat.

So give yourself time. Honour your pace. And listen to the habits that pull you forward, not the ones that hold you back. In the end, our habits are not just actions. They are the invisible threads that stitch together the story of who we are becoming.

<u>Understanding Habitual behaviour:</u>

We don't always notice when a habit begins. One quiet repetition, done without much thought, slowly becomes the path we walk every day. Over time, what once felt like a choice becomes second nature. And this is where the beauty and the danger lies. Habit is both a gift and a warning—a force that can anchor us to purpose or subtly steer us away from it. It doesn't ask for permission. It simply builds itself, one small decision at a time.

Neuroscience calls it efficiency. The brain, always seeking to conserve energy, learns to automate frequent actions. Over time, what we once did with intention becomes reflex;

a morning routine, a reaction to stress, a late-night scroll, a second cup of coffee. These loops shape us far more than we realize.

But not all patterns point us forward. Some hold us in place. Some left unexamined lead us away from the very things we hope to grow into. *Self-sabotage*. Delay. Overindulgence. The cost of an unconscious habit isn't always immediate, but it compounds. Like water carving stone, it reshapes us slowly, then suddenly.

And before a habit can change, it must be seen. Not judged, not fixed—just noticed. Most habits begin as small responses to something deeper: a need, a discomfort, a feeling left unattended. Often, they're not about the habit itself, but about what we were trying to hold together in that moment.

On a more tangible level, every habit follows a pattern: a cue, a routine, and a reward. The cue something we might overlook, signals the start of the habit. It can be an internal feeling like boredom or anxiety, or an external trigger such as a place, a time, or a familiar voice in our minds. Recognizing these cues helps us understand how habits take shape.

When I was living in Ukhrul, Manipur, I found myself drinking cup after cup of black coffee. The cold, the silence, the endless rain; they created a perfect stage. It wasn't about caffeine. It was about comfort. Something warm to hold. Something familiar in a day that felt empty. Only when the restlessness and sleeplessness caught up with me did I begin to ask: *what am I really reaching for?*

That question—what am I reaching for? is often the key. Habits are not problems; they're messengers. And behind every persistent pattern is an unmet need asking to be seen.

Change began not with shame, but with curiosity. I swapped black coffee for herbal tea, hot water, even walks in the rain. Not to deprive myself, but to meet the same need; calm, warmth, grounding in a different way.

On the other hand, positive habits don't just eliminate the negative; they build a new rhythm. In Delhi, I began making my bed each morning; a simple act I picked up from my older brother. *He believed that order in the environment nurtured order in the mind.* He was right. That small ritual helped me begin my day not in chaos, but in clarity. It created a sense of progress before the world even asked anything of me.

What we practice daily becomes the soil our life grows in. And whether we plant intention or inattention makes all the difference. The beauty is, habits don't require inspiration; only repetition. You don't have to feel ready. You just have to begin.

But let's be honest; changing a habit is rarely graceful. It asks for friction. It brings resistance. It requires patience, not performance. And most of all, it calls for compassion. We're not machines rewriting code. We are living beings, learning new ways to care for ourselves.

So let your habits become your allies. Let them carry your values quietly, across the days when motivation wanes. Let them be a soft structure that steadies you, a rhythm that supports the life you are choosing, not the one you're drifting through. We don't rise to the level of our goals; we fall to the strength of our habits. Choose them wisely. Tend to them daily. And remember: every small act of awareness is a step toward becoming someone new.

<u>Overcome procrastination:</u>

When we fall into the wrong habit, procrastination takes root. It doesn't begin with a bold refusal— it begins with a delay. A scroll. A snack. A sudden urge to clean the room instead of facing the task that matters. These small detours, repeated over time, form grooves in our behavior that are hard to notice and even harder to escape.

It's not laziness, not really. Often, it's fear dressed as indifference. Fear of not doing it well enough. Of not being ready. Of what it might say about us if we try and fall short. And so, we postpone. We busy ourselves with what feels easier, more certain. But somewhere deep inside, we know we're bargaining with time and it never forgets the cost.

It was our final year of college, and we were assigned a major field project. The instructions were clear. Our professor encouraged us to begin early, offered guidance, even welcomed our questions. *"There's time,"* he said, *"but only if you use it wisely."* I nodded along, made quiet promises to myself. But somehow, I kept putting it off; not out of laziness, but from something quieter, more familiar. A belief that there was still time. That pressure would make me sharper. That I could afford to wait.

The days passed like leaves in wind. I filled them with everything but the one thing that mattered—long hours with friends, empty scrolls through my phone, distractions that felt harmless until they weren't. Deep down, I knew I was delaying. And yet, I couldn't bring myself to begin. The project became a shadow that followed me—silent, heavy, and growing.

When the deadline finally loomed, it felt like a wave crashing before I'd learned to swim. I stayed up through the nights, chasing lost time with coffee and panic. The work I produced felt rushed, hollow. I submitted it knowing it wasn't what I was capable of. And the worst part wasn't the grade. It was the disappointment I carried afterward; knowing I had more to give, but I'd never given myself the chance.

That experience stayed with me; not as a failure, but as a mirror. Procrastination isn't just about avoiding work; it's often about avoiding emotion. The discomfort of starting. The fear of the unknown. The vulnerability of showing up. And so we create routines that comfort us in the moment but rob us of momentum in the long run.

Yet even patterns that hold us back can be unlearned. With self-awareness, we can begin to recognize the cues, the moment our mind starts to wander, the feeling of resistance rising in our chest. And in that space between awareness and action, we can choose differently. Not perfectly. Just differently. A small step. A quiet beginning. A kind word to ourselves instead of judgment.

At the heart of procrastination is not a failure of effort, but a forgetting of care, a care for our time, our values, and the life we're trying to create. When we remember that, change begins. We start not when we feel ready, but when we remember why it matters. And in those small moments of returning of choosing to begin again, we build habits that support us, not out of pressure, but out of something steadier. Not as punishment, but as a quiet form of self-respect.

Habits to improve self-esteem

Self-esteem isn't something we find all at once, it's something we slowly build, often through steady, deliberate ways. It grows in the small, unseen choices we make every day: how we speak to ourselves in the silence, how we respond to our own mistakes, how gently we treat the parts of us still learning.

When we fall into the wrong habits of self-criticism, comparison, or seeking validation in places that never give; our sense of worth slowly begins to wear thin. These patterns don't always look harmful; yet they quietly shape the way we see ourselves, until doubt feels familiar and confidence like a distant thing. But just as we drift into these unhelpful rhythms, we can also choose new ones. And that choice begins not with pressure, but with permission; to begin again with care. Start small. Tend to yourself like someone you care about. Not perfectly, but consistently. Practice showing up with kindness through self-care that isn't performative but nourishing. Through goals that are realistic and meaningful and not punishing. Through language that uplifts rather than diminishes: *"I am still learning, and that is enough."*

This inner kindness is only part of the story. The people around us—their words, their energy—weave into our sense of self, shaping it in ways both subtle and profound. Clarity didn't arrive in a single moment. It came from listening; not just to others, but to how I felt in their presence. There's wisdom in noticing what lifts you and what wears you down. And sometimes, self-respect begins with choosing distance. Protecting our self-esteem often means re-evaluating the voices we allow into our lives, including our own. We don't need perfection. We need presence, compassion that softens the edges, and the courage to walk away from what no longer helps us grow.

There's wisdom in the saying, *"If you focus on the good, the good gets better."* When we begin to notice the good in ourselves, in others, in the subtle rhythms of our day, we shift our story. Gratitude isn't about ignoring the hard parts. It's about seeing what's still whole, still working, still worthy—even in the midst of becoming.

The power of Positive Habits:

Habits shape us more than we realize, they are the silent stories we tell ourselves each day. Almost half of what we do flows from these hidden patterns, gently tearing the course of our lives. When we choose positive habits, we don't just change what we do, we change who we are. With each choice, we're not just moving, we're becoming. Often, it begins with something almost nothing; a small shift in how we respond, what we notice, or what we choose to hold onto. These small, consistent acts carry great strength. Over time, they begin to change the way we see ourselves and how we meet the world around us.

I've been stubborn too; resistant to change, held tight by comfort. Growing up, I leaned on my parents' support and avoided challenges that pushed me beyond my familiar world. But life, in its own gentle way, nudged me forward. I remember the first time I cooked for myself, the awkwardness and the small victory that followed. That moment was less about food and more about learning to stand on my own. It showed me that even reluctant steps can lead to freedom.

Change often begins awkwardly, unfamiliar, uncomfortable, and unsure. But as we stay with it, the unfamiliar becomes part of us. What once felt distant slowly finds its place in our days.

When habits settle in, they free us from constant struggle. They become the background music of our days; steady, reliable, allowing us to focus on what matters: our passions, loved ones, our peace. This ease is not laziness but a gift—

the brain's way of clearing space so we can be fully present.

Our habits shape our character. If we choose honesty, we build trust; if we choose kindness, we build connection. It's a simple truth, but one that deserves our attention. Each small choice matters. We are not defined by moments of weakness, but by the habits we cultivate over time. Look closely at your habits today. Which ones lift you up? Which ones hold you back? And talk within yourself, it is a conversation between who you are and who you wish to be. Be patient. Be kind to yourself. And remember, every habit is a chance to rewrite your story.

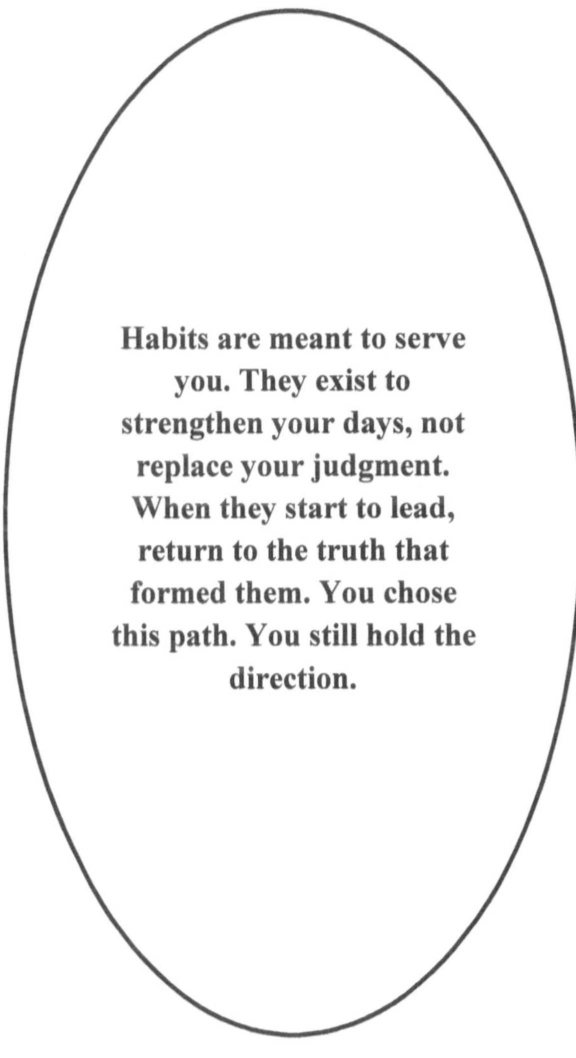

Habits are meant to serve
you. They exist to
strengthen your days, not
replace your judgment.
When they start to lead,
return to the truth that
formed them. You chose
this path. You still hold the
direction.

A flower never asks to be admired; it simply blooms. Yet how we respond to its growth or its beauty says more about us than about the flower itself. Some nurture life until it unfolds; others take beauty the moment it appears. I've come to believe we love the world in the same way; we love people either by staying, or by passing through. In both, the truest language is not in what we say, but in how we tend, see, and sustain.

Let's talk about Like and Love.

What we nurture shapes us. What we show invites judgment. Finding the middle path is how we help others understand us.

I love flowers. I tuck them into pots along the corridor, nestle them inside my home, and scatter green corners wherever I can; in the bedroom, by the windows, even on my desk. There's a quiet joy in watching them grow. Their presence brings a kind of calm that words rarely touch. Even on difficult days, one glance at a blooming flower or a stretch of green is enough to soften the noise in my mind.

On my study desk, I keep a cactus and a snake plant—low-maintenance companions, yet they demand their own kind of care. Every two or three days, I carry them into the light, check if the soil needs water, if the roots are hungry, or if a disease has crept in unnoticed. I clean their leaves, rub a little plant oil to give them a fresh gleam, and yes sometimes, the cactus pricks me. But that sting feels small when I see the tiny spikes thriving, stubborn and alive.

It's not easy, especially here in Delhi, where the air turns heavy and the summer's burn without pause. The pollution doesn't just cloud the sky, it slowly wearies the leaves, dulling their shine and stealing their breath. And still, I try. Check the humidity, move the pots into gentler light, and do what I can to give these lives a fair chance. It takes effort, yes. But somehow, it never feels like a burden. The calm they bring, the comfort of simply being there is always worth more than the work they require.

After a long day, their presence grounds me. I return home tired, drained from hours of working at my desk, staring at the computer, or reading books that stretch the mind and strain the eyes. And there they are my little companions, waiting in stillness, reminding me that peace doesn't have to be something that we seek; it simply exists. Just a glance at my cactus and snake plant, resting on the corner of my desk, gives me a second wind, a soft breath of calm. I don't quite know how, but they do.

But then, there's my sister. She likes flowers too, but not the way I do. I would nurture them, tend to them for weeks, coax them into bloom. She, on the other hand, never watered them, never noticed their needs. But the moment they bloomed, she'd reach for garden scissors or the kitchen knife, snip them at the stem, and place them in a vase. Two days later, they'd wilt, and she'd move on.

The flower was never meant to be severed. It bloomed in the soil, under care, where it belonged. But for her, it was enough to enjoy it for a moment, even if that moment meant its end. And in that difference between us, I saw something—*the meaning of Love and Like or the purpose of Like and Love.*

The way we treat flowers is often the way we treat people. When we **love**, we stay. We nurture. We make space for growth, even when it's inconvenient. We tend to the roots, not just the petals. But when we **like**, we may admire from a distance or worse, take what we want and walk away when the bloom begins to fade.

To love is to build. To like is to borrow beauty. That's why it's so important to understand what others bring into your life; do they love you, or do they merely like you? Do they seek a home in your heart, or just a moment in your presence? In romance, in friendship, in every bond we form, this distinction matters.

Real care doesn't just admire you; it invests in your growth, even in unnoticed ways. Love is not always grand; it isn't something you pick and place in a jar, but something that nurtures you where you belong, like a gardener tending to life. And once we understand that, we stop mistaking brief attention for devotion, or fleeting presence for care.

Every garden inside or outside reflects who we are. What we grow within shapes what the world sees outside.

The Language of Appearance

The way you walk into the world tells a story. Choose to walk as someone who values substance over spectacle.

How we carry ourselves in public; what we wear, how we walk, how we speak tells a silent story to the world. It's not always fair, and it may feel shallow, but in reality: people perceive us through what they see before they understand who we are.

You might call it judgment. You might call it instinct. But either way, it shapes how strangers respond to us.

Think of this: what would you think if someone wore a bikini to a church or temple. Or a formal suit to a beach party? No matter the intent, they'll draw puzzled looks—maybe whispers. It wouldn't be about the person's character, it would be about the mismatch between appearance and environment. And this mismatch makes people uncomfortable. That discomfort quickly turns to judgment. Our clothing, our behavior, our very presence speaks a language, and that language is deeply tied to context. Clothes don't just cover the body; they communicate.

A bikini on a beach is normal. But a bikini in a place of worship? Suddenly, it's a statement. A suit in a boardroom is expected. A suit on a beach feels misplaced.

When we step into public spaces, we don't arrive alone. We carry with us a set of signals; clothing, posture, and tone that people decode within seconds. Whether we like it or not, this decoding happens constantly.

I live in Delhi, where the summers are relentless. At home, I keep it simple; light clothes, comfort first. I don't mind when people around me do the same. If my sister wears shorts at home, I don't blink; that's our comfort zone. But outside, it's a different story. Not because she's wrong, but because the world isn't always kind.

She might wear something just to beat the heat. But out there, others might not see her intent. They might only see her body. And their judgments often crude, often baseless, will have nothing to do with who she truly is. Unfortunately, not everyone outside carries innocence in their eyes and not everyone deserve the benefit of the doubt.

Society tends to speak in the voice of the majority:

- *If you dress differently, you may be labeled immodest.*
- *If you speak differently, you may be seen as difficult.*
- *If you act differently, you may be misunderstood.*
- *If you believe differently, you may be silenced.*

The majority often doesn't pause to ask who you are. It simply reacts to who you appear to be.

Appearance is a language, and society is quick to translate, even when it misunderstands. A person in a school uniform is assumed to be a student, even if it's just a costume for a drama or a house party. A police uniform commands respect, even if it's worn for a movie scene. A confident speaker is taken for an expert, even when the words are scripted. And a hesitant voice, trembling, and unsure one is often overlooked, even when it carries hard-won wisdom. We're not always seen for who we are. More often, we're seen for what we appear to be.

Perception is powerful and flawed.

If you want to sink in more into experience, try something. Dress in a way that defies the norm just once and step into a familiar public space. Watch the way people look at you, how they respond. Then, another day, dress the way society expects. You'll see the difference. Same person, different reactions. It's not you who's changed; it's the lens through which you're being seen.

Now, this isn't a call to conform blindly or live in fear of judgment. You don't owe the world an explanation for every choice. But awareness isn't submission, its strategy. Knowing how the world sees helps you walk through it with intention. So yes, be yourself. Wear what feels true to you. Speak your truth. But also understand where you are, and who's watching, not to shrink yourself, but to choose, with clarity, when and how you wish to be seen, and in what light. People often don't respond to you, they respond to the version of you they've created in their minds. And once you know that, you can choose your presentation not from fear, but from clarity.

<u>**Note:**</u>

- ♠ *The way we care reveals the depth of our love. The way we appear reveals the assumptions we invite.*
- ♠ *To be seen is easy. To be understood—now that takes intention.*
- ♠ *Like may cut the flower for its beauty; love waters the roots for its life.*

Before love finds us, life teaches us to see with clarity, to listen with patience, and to choose with intention. It guides us through longing, missteps, and reflection, shaping how we come to understand connection. Only then does love become more than desire or fleeting emotion. It transforms into something deeper, a steady current that points us toward growth, understanding, and the life we are meant to share.

Choose your boyfriend wisely

Look for the one who turns ordinary days into safe places, who doesn't just love you, but knows how to carry life with you.

We are given two lives; the first, the life we inherit from our parents, and the second, the life we craft through the choices we make. Among these choices, none feels as defining as the decision of choosing a life partner. It is a choice that shapes the stories we tell ourselves about love, trust, and companionship. Your partner will become the keeper of your emotions, your companion through the seasons of life, and the heart of the home you will build together.

You already carry within you the strength of agency; the freedom to choose, to wait, to walk away, or to welcome someone in. But sometimes, that freedom deserves a gentle reminder. Not because you lack it, but because its impact is so profound. The person you choose will not just share your days, but your dreams. Not just your moments, but the subtle truths they carry.

They become the foundation upon which the heart of our future home is built. They will walk with you, not just through the present, but into a future yet unseen. They will shape the home your heart longs to build. And so, the one you choose matters, not just for who they are today, but for who they are willing to become beside you.

To choose wisely is not to rush or settle. It is to honor your own worth, to listen inward, and to stay true to the vision you carry for the life ahead. When you begin to understand your worth, love itself begins to change shape; it becomes less about finding someone and more about recognizing who truly resonates with your becoming.

What if the person you choose understands the language of your true self; the hopes that stretch beyond the present moment? Not just the desires of today, but the dreams you carry for your future self and the family you desire for the future. Could this person be someone you admire, who sees you, truly sees you, and wishes to grow with you, hand in hand, for a lifetime?

Such love is beautiful, but it also calls for discernment. For in the pursuit of connection, we sometimes forget the boundaries that protect our peace and preserve our becoming.

There is a gentle warning to carry with you:

- ♠ *Don't trade your future for your present cravings.*
- ♠ *Don't confuse your wants with your needs.*
- ♠ *Don't exchange your values just to escape loneliness.*

You deserve so much more than fleeting pleasures and immediate gratification. Your worth is far greater than the temporary pleasures and immediate gratification that come with a partner who doesn't meet your long-term desires. You were made perfect in your becoming. The more you look within, the more you will realize your magnificence and worthiness. Your unique looks, personality, loving heart, character, and talent make you the priceless jewel you are.

Before inviting another into your life, spend time with yourself. Discover the depths of your worth, so you may recognize what really belongs beside you. Love, much like choice, requires clarity of feeling, knowing what aligns with your inner-self.

Imagine choosing clothes, not simply by the glitter of the fabric on a hanger, but by the feel of the garment against your skin, the way it moves with you, and the comfort it brings. And with that same tenderness, choose your partner, not for surface beauty or fleeting attraction, but for the harmony that fits your soul and the dreams you carry.

Ask yourself these:

- What do you have in common with this person?
- How does this person reflect the future you desire?
- When you're vulnerable, does he hold space for you?
- Does his presence feel peaceful or dominating?

Ask yourself honestly and reflect on these questions to ensure that the person you choose as a partner aligns with your true desires and the future you envision for yourself. Ask whether the person has the qualities that will contribute to your overall relationship and happiness in the long run.

If a person's qualities are not aligned with your long-term desires and values, it is wiser for you to let go and seek a more compatible partner. That is the easy solution to long-term stress and dissatisfaction in a relationship. Don't let today's choices become tomorrow's regrets by settling for someone who is not the right fit for you. Be wise enough to understand the person you want to spend your life with and understand their other side of the story and their intentions. Notice how he treats those who hold no power over him. Observe the subtleties in his actions; the respect he shows, the honesty he carries, and the loyalty he lives by. True character reveals itself over time, and often in the moments when no one is watching.

Don't take it lightly by just saying, *'We'll figure it out,'* or by ignoring red flags and thinking, *'I'll change him.'* You can't reshape a grown person to fit your ideals—it's like trying to straighten a mature bent tree. Core values forged over years rarely bend; They may change slyly to please you temporarily, but ultimately, their true nature will resurface, and the incompatibilities may become more pronounced over time.

To truly know someone, look beyond what they say, observe what shapes them. Notice the influences that guide their choices, the friendships that reflect their values, and the habits that reveal their priorities. Every life carries traces of where it has been and what it holds dear. Stability, honesty, and respect are not words we claim, they are patterns we live. The way a person treats time, people, and promises tells you more than any confession of love ever could. True character is not announced; it is revealed, *through overtime*.

The Mirror of Love

A queen does not seek a crown, she seeks a king. For loyalty meets loyalty and love recognizes its own reflection.

Love is reciprocal; those who are faithful and kind will seek the same in you. They notice the respect you show, the trust you inspire, and the care you offer to those around you. If your actions and values align, a lasting bond is possible; if not, the relationship may falter.

Think of the partner you hope to share your life with. What qualities matter most? And what qualities do you offer in return? Imagine the life you wish to build together, and the example you hope to set for the next generation. Every choice you make today, how you treat yourself, how you honour your values, all these plants seeds for the relationship you hope to nurture tomorrow. Nurture wisely, and love can bloom. Neglect what matters and you might end up harvesting the weeds.

The Emotional Predator–Spot and Stop the Cycle

Even as we seek love, not all hearts we encounter will honour it. Some individuals—regardless of gender—may exploit vulnerability for personal gain, whether for attention, control, or validation. Like foxes circling their prey, they study your fears, desires, and kindness, and use them to create a false sense of intimacy. Their pattern is familiar: flattery, hot-and-cold attention, and just enough sincerity to keep you engaged until they withdraw, leaving confusion in their wake.

What makes this dangerous isn't only manipulation; it's how it targets our deepest needs. Everyone longs for connection, and predators recognize that. They may amplify insecurities or offer a vision of love that serves them more than you; one that feels comforting at first, then it slowly begins to take more than it gives. The aftermath? Doubt, disillusionment, and emotional weariness.

Protect yourself by looking for consistency, not promises. Watch for gaps between words and actions. Do they honour your boundaries? Do they invest in your happiness? Real love does not hide in ambiguity, it is patient, steady, and truthful.

Unseen Doesn't Mean Unworthy

You are like a diamond; not because someone must appraise you to give you value, but because your worth is innate, unchangeable, and radiant on its own. A diamond doesn't lose its brilliance when placed in the wrong hands, it simply waits for those who recognize its true nature. In the same way, if someone fails to cherish you, it doesn't mean you lack value. It only means they lack the clarity to see it.

Remember this:

- ♠ ***Your worth was never negotiable.*** *Like a diamond's atomic structure, it cannot be altered or diminished.*
- ♠ ***The right love doesn't test your value, it reflects.*** *Like a master jeweller, they'll know how to honour your rarity.*

When someone fails to see your value, it says everything about their vision and nothing about your radiance.

This isn't about demanding others to "see your worth," it's about never forgetting it yourself. When you stop questioning if you're enough, you start recognizing who is enough for you. A diamond doesn't chase after those who mistake it for glass. It simply stays, luminous and sure, until the right light finds it. *So do you!*

Financial Independence

Your partner may one day be the father of your children. But **"father"** is more than a role; it is a presence, strength, or a compass in storms of life. Not just someone who shares your laughter, but someone who helps carry the weight of the days.

And so, it matters that he stands on his own feet. That he isn't waiting for life to begin, but is already building something with intention. Even if his hands are still gathering, his eyes should know where they're headed.

Financial independence isn't about numbers in a bank. I''s about, responsibility, discipline and of someone who understands the balance between today's joy and tomorrow's needs. All this, You'll notice it in how he treats what he earns, how he honours what he has, how he speaks of the future, not as a distant dream, but as something he's already shaping.

Some drift, cushioned by others. Some earn, but spend like time won't catch up. Neither may be ready, not because they're unkind, but because they haven't yet learned what it means to hold steady for more than just themselves.

So look, not with judgment, but with openness. Does he move with purpose? Does he carry the kind of ambition that is reliable? Not ambition for status; but for depth, for wholeness, for something that can last. Because love—real love—needs more than feeling. It needs a place to root. And it flourishes in the soil of stability, trust, and shared vision.

So ask yourself, not as a test, but as a truth: **Is he drifting, or becoming? Is he merely passing through the present, or patiently preparing for the life he longs to live?** In the end, it's not the sweet words that hold love together, but the small, steady ones—the ones that say, *"I'm here. I'm building. I'm with you!"*

<u>Looks matter.</u>

****Beauty begins the story, but character writes the ending.*

Yes, looks catch the eye; but it's the soul that holds your gaze when the world quiets down. Attraction begins at the surface, but love—real love—asks for more. It asks you to see not just how someone appears, but how they carry their days, how they speak when no one is watching, and whether their presence feels like home.

There's a kind of beauty that doesn't fade with time; it lives in character, in kindness, in the subtle strength of someone who listens, stays, and grows. You see it in how they make you feel safe to be yourself, in the ways they care without needing to be seen.

Many fall for the glitter of what's visible; only to find, too late, that it held no weight. And yet, when you're seen and understood for who you are and not just how you look, you discover something far rarer: ***resonance*** a soul-deep connection where affection meets meaning, and hearts can unfold without fear.

Physical attraction has its place, but let it be a doorway, not the destination. Beyond it, ask:
Does this person know how to listen?
Do we laugh in the same language?
Do we want to walk in the same direction—even if the path isn't always smooth?

A relationship that endures isn't built only in candlelight; it's built in morning coffees, shared silences, difficult conversations, and the grace to begin again. It's built in choosing each other, even when life grows heavy.

As you turn these pages of *A Love Letter to My Sister*, remember this: There's a saying: *You learn nothing from the cover, it's the pages within that teach you who someone truly is.* And the same is true of love. Looks may spark the story, drawing you in at first glance, but it's what lies beneath the unspoken truths, the shared dreams, the hidden depths, that write the chapters worth keeping.

So let your heart be drawn, **yes**, but let it also be discerning. Seek not only someone beautiful to look at, but someone beautiful to build with. Someone whose presence feels like peace, whose spirit, not just their face, lights up your world. The glow that lasts isn't always seen; it's felt. And that's the kind of love that stays.

We do not heal by turning away from our pain or pretending it does not exist. True healing begins when we face it fully, sitting with it until it loses its power to frighten us. It is in that openness, in simply allowing what it is, that we find the strength to move forward.

How I Sit with My Emotions

"The wound is the place where the light enters you." –

Rumi

Last week, I felt myself slipping. My thoughts were tangled, and even the simplest tasks—writing, working, just breathing, all felt difficult. I kept hoping that pushing through would help, but the more I tried, the heavier it became. Every small mistake frustrated me; every distraction reminded me that I couldn't fully control my mind. Some days, just forming a clear sentence felt impossible, and the weight inside seemed to grow with every effort.

People often say, *'Go for a walk. Be around friends. It helps.'* And yes, for a moment, it does. I feel better when I am around my friends and when I go for a walk, but the healing is temporary. Once I return to my usual routine, the negative emotions start to creep in, and everything feels overwhelming again. And yet, the truth is, people can't walk beside me forever. They have their own lives, their own journeys and I can't ask them to pause for mine.

That's when I began to understand something: healing is an inward journey. No one can walk it for me. The battle is not just against the emotions, but in learning how to meet them. It's not about erasing the sadness, or silencing the stress, or pretending the frustration isn't there. It's about facing the raw, difficult parts of who we are with honesty and care.

Whatever we carry; grief from a broken relationship, pressure from work, the ache of not being where we hoped to be, it must be acknowledged. Not judged. Not rushed away. Just felt, gently and truthfully, allowed to surface without shame. Much like muddy water in a bucket, if we allow stillness—if we stop stirring and simply let it be, the murk begins to settle. And in time, what was once cloudy becomes clear again. Only then do we begin to see clearly, to discern what is meant to stay and what must be released.

Healing doesn't ask us to hurry. It asks only for honesty. A willingness to say, *'Yes, this is here. Yes, this is mine.'* And in that recognition, the emotion begins to soften—not all at once, but like water slowly clearing on its own.

The world may not pause, but you can. You can listen to yourself without interruption. You can give your hurt a name, a little space. And sometimes, in that stillness, something shifts. Sometimes, that's where the healing begins.

I usually rely on two methods to calm my negative emotions.

Meditation: 01

There are days when the heaviness becomes too much; when I can't seem to find peace, when anger clouds every thought, and I feel lost in a storm I didn't ask for. In those moments, I retreat. I seek a quiet place where I can be alone with myself, undisturbed.

I close the door to my room, sit down in my chair, and put on soft music through my earphones. Then I close my eyes and invite my mind to wander into a serene world, the one that mirrors the sounds I hear. If the music carries the hush of nature, I imagine myself walking through a lush forest. I can feel the cool breeze on my skin, hear the birds singing beside a river, and listen to the soft gurgle of water flowing over stones.

In that imagined, something in me softens. The noise within begins to settle, like a bucket of stirred water left untouched, the turmoil within slowly begins to sink. Each breath grows steadier. The heaviness I carry doesn't vanish, but it loosens its grip. As if the forest, in all its gentleness, knows how to hold what I cannot yet release.

Once I feel a little more grounded, I gently turn my attention to the situation that has been troubling me. I revisit the memory—not to relive it with judgment, but to witness it with awareness. I allow myself to feel what I felt: the anger, the hurt, the confusion. I do not silence them. I simply sit with them, like old friends who showed up unannounced, asking only to be acknowledged.

Then, I speak inwardly:

- ✓ I have seen the truth of it.
- ✓ I have felt the weight of it.
- ✓ I have understood what it came to teach me.

And *I will never let this happen to me again in the future.*

But I don't stop at setting boundaries. I offer myself grace.

- ✓ For having the courage to face what hurt.
- ✓ For choosing clarity over avoidance.
- ✓ For bringing peace to a storm that once controlled me.

This way, I express gratitude to myself for what I've learned and achieved through this experience, while also setting boundaries to prevent similar situations in the future.

> **Note:** *Treat your emotions as you would a lover—free them from the prison of your judgment. Let them dance around you, wrap around your heart, and transform them into something beautiful.*

<u>**Writing: 02**</u>

When my heart feels cluttered and my thoughts are spinning, I turn to the page. Writing becomes another mirror, a release and a quiet witness.

I sit at my desk, turn on my laptop, open a blank document, and let the words come, unfiltered and unruly. I don't worry about grammar or making sense. I simply pour out my unsettled mind; sadness, anger, questions, longings, and all the pieces I haven't yet found the words for.

When the screen is full, I read back what I've written, allowing myself to truly see the emotions laid bare before me. In those lines, patterns begin to emerge. I find the roots of old wounds, the tangled threads I didn't realize were still holding on. Seeing my emotions clearly, I can accept them, not as burdens to fight, but as parts of myself with needs and stories waiting to be understood.

<u>**Warning:**</u> *If you are not comfortable or familiar with expressing your emotions through writing, then I suggest you not force yourself to do it. Instead, find other methods of self-expression that resonate with you, such as meditation, art, or doing something that makes you feel calm and grounded.*

Here are some ways my friends cope with negative emotions.

1) **Dancing:** One of my friends, **Mary**, told me when she's overwhelmed, she locks herself into her room and puts on music that moves her. She will dance until she feels the weight of her negative emotions lifts.

2) **Temple:** Another friend, Vishnu, finds solace in visiting the **Gurudwara** (*a Sikh temple*). She spends time sitting beside the **Sarovar** (the sacred lake beside the temple), absorbing its positive energy—a form of meditation for her.

3) **Walking with her dog:** Another friend shared that her go-to method for coping with negative emotions is taking her dog for walks in a nearby park. She finds peace and relief in her dog's companionship.

*(You might be wondering why I'm not including **"talking to friends"** as one of the ways to deal with negative emotions. Yes! Talking to friends can certainly be a helpful way to reduce negative emotions at times, but you see most of our friends are not our forever, and sometimes the people we consider our best friend can be our worst enemy. So sharing your emotions with your enemy is like putting gas in the fire). Here, I am also not saying that talking to friends is always a bad idea, but it's important to choose the right people to confide in and ensure that they are trustworthy. Or in other words don't play **Ludo** (luck) with your emotions.)*

Each of us must find our own language for healing, whether through meditation, writing, walking, or simply sitting with the rawness of what we feel. There is no universal remedy, no shortcut to peace. But there is always a way to understand, to feel, and to move through what hurts with honesty. Avoidance may offer brief relief, yet true peace begins when we return to ourselves without any judgment.

***What you avoid will remain. What you face can transform.*

Life has its way of showing us that love was never meant to be kept; it was meant to be lived. It endures as we grow and change.

My love for you has Its Seasons

The world may tempt you with bright things, yet your actions today speak into your tomorrow.

My love for you has always been constant, but like the seasons, it will change its form, even if not in its depth. I don't say this with coldness. It aches even to write these words. But you need to know this, not because I want distance between us, but because I love you enough to speak the truth: there will come a point when our paths naturally begin to diverge. And I need you to understand that this isn't about growing apart emotionally, it's about growing into who we're meant to become, and the responsibilities that come with it.

One day, you will fall in love. You'll choose someone to walk beside you, and you'll begin a life that is fully yours. You'll build a home, grow into your own world of love, work, and responsibility, and slowly, naturally, the role I play in your life will begin to change. And when that happens, I won't hold it against you that my place in your life shifts. In fact, I'll celebrate it—even from afar.

If life is kind; as it often is, in ways we only come to see later, I will have my own family, my own responsibilities. My time, my focus, my heart will be stretched across new roles, and I may not always be able to show up for you in the same ways I do now. It's not because I'll love you any less—it's simply that my role will evolve, as it should be.

Love can remain steady, even as its shape begins to shift. Now I see this more clearly: it's not a disappearance, but a transformation. It's love learning to grow alongside life's demands, perhaps, but no less real.

This is not a sad thing. This is life doing what life does: teaching us to love in deeper, quieter, more sacrificial ways.

We've seen this before, haven't we? In our parents. Once, they were just like us—siblings sharing laughter, food, and stories. But life moved forward. They married, had us, and their lives began to revolve around their own homes. That's not abandonment, its love choosing where it's most needed. It's the wisdom of knowing we can't give everything to everyone. It matured.

Think about it: if our parents gave more time and care to their siblings' children than to us, would it feel fair? And if our uncles and aunts neglected their own children to look after us, would that really be love? Love is not about giving equally—it's about giving rightly.

There's a sacred responsibility in caring for the people who rely on you. Even the old teachings, like **Grihastha Dharma** emphasize this. They remind us that once we step into that chapter of life, the home we build must become the center of our efforts. It means that our love doesn't disappear; it just learns where it is most needed.

I say all this because I want you to be prepared, not just for the emotional shift, but for life itself. Don't be caught off guard by the way priorities will change. Instead while this season still belongs to us, I want you to live fully. Let this be your time to build yourself from the inside out. Not just with books or degrees, but with wisdom. With patience. With self-respect. Learn to enjoy your own company, to listen when life whispers, to guard your focus, and to give your energy only to what nourishes your future. Don't treat these years lightly. They are the soil for everything you will become.

Learn what will help you grow. Learn to value your time, your attention, and your energy. Not everything that looks urgent is important, and not everything that's pleasurable will take you somewhere worth going. This is your moment to become the person your future will thank you for.

Don't lose this chance. Don't let distraction dress itself as freedom. Don't trade a strong future for fleeting comfort. The seeds you plant now, through your effort will become the foundation of everything that's coming. It's not just about studying hard or setting goals. It's about learning to care for your own life with seriousness and grace.

You won't get to blame others forever. You won't be able to say, *"I failed because my parents didn't support me,"* or *"I didn't have time,"* or *"my friends held me back."* In the end, your life will be the result of your choices. Your future won't accept excuses—it will only reflect the truth of your daily actions. So don't take the easy way out. Don't make room for laziness, for unkind self-talk, or for people who dull your spirit. Reject anything that doesn't honour who you are trying to become.

And most of all fall deeply in love with yourself, not in vanity, but in trust, in curiosity, in care. Know yourself well enough to protect your dreams, even when others don't understand them. Respect yourself enough to walk away from anything that doesn't align with the life you're trying to build.

This is your time. Use it wisely. And know that even when life changes, my love for you will always remain faithfully in a different season.

<u>NOTE:</u>

> ➤ *Embrace life's possibilities and prepare for its journey with understanding and readiness.*
> ➤ *Fall in love with knowledge and the process of becoming your best self under the guidance of family.*
> ➤ *Reject what adds no value, sacrificing the trivial for a future of significance and success.*
> ➤ *Your future is shaped by today's choices and actions; sow seeds of dedication and reap success.*
> ➤ *Don't let excuses overshadow your potential; take responsibility for shaping your own path.*

There will be moments when the world seems to turn against you, when loss feels endless and the path ahead invisible. But strength is not only in victory, it lives in the choice to keep moving, to hold your heart open, and to keep building the life only you can live. Even in darkness, your light matters.

The Coffee Shop Window

I watched a movie today not because I was searching for meaning, just to pass the time. But somehow, the story reached past the screen and stayed with me. To be very frank, I only clicked on it because the woman was so beautiful——not for the plot, but for the way she turns her head, the way her eyes hold something soft and sincere. **(LoL, that woman even caught me.)**

In a town where time moved slowly, like the rustle of autumn leaves across cobbled streets, there lived a woman known to all for her beauty, but more so for her kindness. Her name, soft as a breeze, lingered in conversations at every tea stall and street corner. Children smiled wider when she passed. Old men straightened their backs in her presence. Her laughter was the town's morning song.

She stood about 5'8", graceful and elegant like poetry walking through the world. Her skin held the warmth of almond and honey, and in sunlight, it seemed to glow like morning dew catching gold. Her hair, thick and gently wavy, flowed in chestnut cascades, usually tied back with a ribbon or scarf that matched the season.

But it wasn't just how she looked, it was the way she *was*.

When she entered a room, it wasn't noise she brought—it was calm. She moved slowly, thoughtfully, as if her body listened to music no one else could hear. Her voice—low, velvety—seemed to still the air, as if time itself leaned in to listen.

Nestled between whispering hills and winding stone paths, the town felt smaller, softer, when she was near. Not just for her beauty, but for something rarer—her presence.

The old men near the coffee shop's window came each morning partly for the brew, but more for the moment she'd greet them by name, placing an extra cookie on the saucer like an old secret. Elderly women paused her mid-shift just to feel the softness of her hands and ask how her garden bloomed so brightly, even in late autumn.

Young boys straightened their posture when she passed. Girls watched her walk and imagined becoming like her someday, not because she wore expensive clothes (*she didn't*), but because she carried herself with dignity stitched to kindness.

Even the stray cats seemed to wait outside the shop during her shift, napping against the warm bricks, as if drawn to the gentle hush she radiated.

She worked at the town's only café, a cozy place with chipped blue tables and the scent of cinnamon and baked oranges in the air. The sign outside was faded, but inside it always felt like home, because she was there. She knew how to make people feel seen. She remembered stories, not just faces. She noticed when someone's eyes were red or their laughter was a little too loud to be real.

She was the kind of woman who made silence feel like companionship

And then, the story turns.

One late afternoon, as the sun dipped low and spilled amber across the hills, a sleek black car broke down near the shop. Out stepped a man whose name was more shadow than sound in the town's streets. They called him a leader, but he ruled not with vision, but with fear. A man who had everything money could buy, and nothing money couldn't.

He entered the cafe to wait for his car to be repaired and saw her.

She approached with a pen and notepad in hand, offering the same smile she gave to every customer. But to him, it felt like something ancient and holy. Her presence disarmed him. Her beauty, yes, but also her warmth, her ease, her quiet confidence.

She didn't recognize who he was. She didn't care.

He was used to women melting under the weight of his reputation. She only offered him a cup of tea.

He became obsessed.

At first, it was gifts and flattery. He tried to court her, win her. But she refused, always with grace. She told him plainly that she was married and loved her husband dearly. Her eyes did not waver. Her voice did not tremble.

But to a man who had never been told **No**, her resistance wasn't a boundary, it was a challenge. He began to circle her life like a storm cloud. And one day, she vanished.

No one saw her leave. But everyone knew who had taken her.

Her husband searched. Day after day, he roamed the edges of the world he could reach. He was no fighter, no warrior, just a man with his heart in pieces, trying to hold on to love. But the man who had taken her was untouchable. He held the city in his pocket. And no amount of pleading or justice could break through.

And she? She waited. In quiet hours and restless nights, she whispered his name like a prayer. She watched the seasons change from behind locked windows, hoping to see his shadow on the coffee shop. Twice she tried to run; once through the gardens, once through the servants' gate, but each time, the walls proved taller than her will and the city colder than her fear. Her longing ached, but she was trapped in a life that wasn't hers, bound by choices she never made.

Meanwhile, in the marble halls of the mansion on the hill, she lived as a prisoner.

The bad leader took her as his wife, but only in name. And yet, he didn't touch her. He gave her everything he knew to offer—flowers she never asked for, books he hoped would soften her solitude, silence when words felt like trespass. Behind the cold marble walls of the mansion, he gave her space—his clumsy way of love. At first, she thought it was a trick, a trap. But time passed, and the man who had always taken began to fumble toward giving. *Not perfectly. Not gracefully*. But honestly. Like a child learning to walk, he stumbled through kindness, unsure, untrained but trying. Because for the first time, he wanted to be worthy, not feared.

She saw him helping an old man carrying loads. She heard rumors; he donated money to rebuild the town's school, the library, the broken bridge. He began doing what he never had before—*he listened!*

He didn't know how to love, but he wanted to learn.

Still, she did not forgive. But the months past, and the seasons slowly favouring her to get closer to him and out of love she bore him a child. A baby girl with her mother's eyes and the softness of dawn in her cheeks. And something began to shift. The woman who once belonged to everyone now belonged to one thing only: *her daughter*.

Even in captivity, she held to her grace. She sang lullabies by the moonlight. She taught the child words that tasted like love. And though she could not forgive the man who caged her, she could not hate the child who had her smile.

The bad leader, surprisingly, became a doting father. He built nurseries out of gold and filled the rooms with laughter. And while her heart still bore the scars of violence, she saw something she hadn't expected: **a tiny piece of peace** in the eyes of her daughter.

She stayed not because she surrendered, but because she couldn't abandon the one thing still untouched by sorrow: her daughter.

Each night, she held the child close, humming lullabies woven from memory and longing, whispering a name that still lived like fire in her chest: her husband's.

And somewhere beyond the stone walls, her ex-husband watched.
Not up close, he couldn't, but from a distance that only heartbreak understands.
He saw her smile, now dimmed but still there.
He saw the man beside her, holding the child that wasn't his and yet somehow was.
He didn't know her captivity.

He couldn't hear her silent pleas.
But he felt the weight of her absence like a ghost lying beside him at night.

One morning, as mist curled over the river they once danced beside under stars,
he stepped into the water; not to escape, but to remember.
Each step a memory. Each ripples a goodbye.
When the current touched his chest, he closed his eyes and let go, letting his soul drift with the river water.

The story ends here.

At first glance, the story may seem disappointing. The hero gave up, the villain claimed the prize, and life went on without justice or redemption. But perhaps that's the point; it leaves a question burning in its unjust ending. What would you do if you were the one inside that story?

Would you surrender when the world turns its back, when the person or purpose you held dear now belongs to another? Would you let despair carry you into silence, or would you fight, not with rage, but with resolve? Not for a guarantee, but because love, like purpose, is worth the climb.

What if the wife in the story wasn't a person at all, but your calling, your dream, the life you long to build? And the man who took her—what if he was your fear, your doubt, your excuses dressed as circumstance? The truth is, we all face that same question: Do we yield to what seems lost, or do we rise to reclaim what matters?

The path forward won't be easy. It rarely is. But it's still yours. Even if you walk alone, even if no one claps or notices or believes in your comeback, you still hold the pen. Careers can falter, dreams can drift, and even love can stray, but the story is not over until you decide it is.

So fight not with bitterness but with belief. Rebuild not from pride but from purpose. Love not only what you lost but who you are becoming. The obstacles feel real, yes, yet your strength is real too. You were not made to surrender. You were made to rise. Somewhere ahead, a life waits that only you can live.

<table>
<tr><td>

<u>Note:</u>

➢ *Choose resilience over surrender; fight for your dreams as fiercely as you would for your love.*

➢ *Your journey is defined by the choices you make today; choose perseverance, choose victory.*

➢ *Don't let setbacks define you; let your resilience pave the way to a triumphant future.*

➢ *Even in the face of despair, remember: your determination shapes your destiny.*

➢ *The path to greatness requires facing fears head-on and pushing beyond your limits.*

</td></tr>
</table>

We can plan for the future, but life only happens where our feet already rest. The past cannot be rewritten, and the future cannot be entered early. Each moment carries its own meaning, waiting for us to notice it. True life is not in what comes next, but in how fully we embrace the moment we are in.

The Distance between Now and Next

We can shape our future, but we cannot change our past. What we can change is how we carry it. Each choice made now softens what once felt fixed, turning regret into understanding and memory into direction. The past may explain us, yet it does not have the final word. Meaning is not found by rewriting what was, but by living more fully in what still unfolds.

As was his habit, Thuirei set out for his evening jog through the familiar streets of his neighborhood. Ahead, on a dimly lit stretch of the walkway some forty or fifty meters away, he noticed a figure with a face that appeared unusual, almost indistinct.

Curiosity stirred. He walked faster, then faster still, until his body fell into a trot without his consent. The figure ahead drew his focus inward, tightening his attention. The streets receded into the background, familiar turns passing unseen. By the time he finally caught up, his chest burned, his breath ragged, his body drained.

That evening differed from all the others. He did not notice the calm charm of the streets, the quiet pleasure of people on evening walks, the soft consolation of fading light. His awareness had collapsed into a single point, fixed on a stranger whose meaning he did not yet know. The present dissolved while he chased a future that remained undefined.

When he finally saw the person clearly, the revelation was simple. Just an ordinary passerby. Nothing more. The cost, however, was not. In pursuit of a fleeting curiosity, Thuirei had surrendered the fullness of his daily ritual, trading richness for haste, presence for pursuit.

<u>Interpretation</u>

When attention hardens into rigid focus, it risks eroding the meaning of the journey itself. We rarely notice how easily life slips through our grasp when we concentrate solely on achieving a specific objective, neglecting the many experiences that make up the present moment. In chasing the stranger, Thuirei forfeited the richness of his routine, inadvertently trading his immediate experience for a singular, ultimately unfulfilling pursuit.

The figure he follows carries no real significance. Its power exists only in the meaning Thuirei assigns to it. By the time he reaches the stranger, the discovery feels hollow, revealing how often effort is spent running toward something undefined, imagined, or overstated.

Our lives often mirror this inner pattern, where the pursuit of an elusive goal eclipses the very value of the present. We become absorbed in idealized futures or imagined resolutions, failing to notice the subtle beauty and wisdom embedded in everyday moments.

As we grow older, we are bound by ambition, priorities, and an ever expanding list of responsibilities that compel us to look ahead, often at the expense of honoring the journey itself. We mistake our responsibilities for destiny, forgetting that they are temporary roles that shape us without defining our existence. This constant fixation on an imagined future gradually becomes the very antagonist of our lives.

- ✓ We neglect our health, assuming we will care for it once we retire.
- ✓ We neglect our relationships, believing we will mend them when time becomes more generous.
- ✓ We neglect our present well-being, trusting that happiness will arrive after some future success.

More often than not, these expectations become the very reasons we fail to live fully. They turn into unseen restraints, binding us to an endless cycle of dissatisfaction. We miss the fullness of youth while chasing an undefined future, only to discover later that the future is nothing more than a continuation of the present. When the time finally comes to share memories with the young, we realize we skipped the very life we were meant to live.

Perhaps you search for meaning so much that you don't have time to find the answer.

Wisdom plans ahead, but presence gives life its meaning.

Indeed, our future matters, and it is wise to plan for it, but the meaning of life lies in the present, not in the future. We cannot escape the present and live in the future, nor can we relive the past. As it is said, "life is a journey, not a destination." We must learn the meaning of our journey and learn to enjoy every moment we pass through. just like an avid traveler who savors the scenery and local culture rather than fixating solely on the destination, we must also learn to immerse ourselves fully in each step of our existence, appreciating the nuances and lessons each moment offers.

Make a plan for your future, but don't let those plans overshadow the present moment. pursue the career you want, give your best to your work, and honor your commitments, but remember that life's profoundest joys often reside in the unscrepted moments and the connections forged along the way, rather than solely in the fulfillment of future aspirations.

Imagine a father handing his child one hundred rupees to buy a kilogram of apples. In the first instance, the instruction is strict. Buy the apples. Return immediately. Bring back every remaining rupee.

In the second instance, the father gives the same one hundred rupees and the same task, but this time the father's tone is different. Buy the apple, and you may keep the change as you wish.

Which child would feel more empowered and experience greater joy in the execution of their task? The first child, operating under rigid constraints, would likely experience the task as a burden, whereas the second would find pleasure in the autonomy and the opportunity to exercise personal judgment. Similarly, the freedom to engage with the present, rather than being strictly tethered to future outcomes, enables a richer, more meaningful engagement with life's unfolding narrative. In much the same way, when we are not tethered solely to future outcomes, our engagement with life becomes richer and more meaningful. Our existence, like the child given a flexible mandate, grows fuller when we allow ourselves the psychological space to appreciate the present, rather than devoting all attention to what lies ahead.

The ancient Greeks viewed the past as visible before them and the future as unseen behind them. Adopting a similar perspective invites us to reframe our relationship with time. Such a shift encourages momentary living, nurtures a gentler balance between present and future, and eases the sense of alienation born from constant anticipation.

The future will always stand a few steps ahead, inviting pursuit, demanding preparation. It never waits to be lived. Life only happens where our feet already rest.

Thuirei never lost anything tangible that evening. No time, no money, no opportunity. Yet something essential slipped away. The warmth of familiar streets. The unremarkable beauty of routine. The quiet dignity of being present. All traded for a moment that revealed nothing new. This is how life often passes us. Not through tragedy or failure, but through attention misplaced. We run toward what we imagine matters, while meaning unfolds unnoticed at our side. The tragedy is subtle. By the time we look back, the road we rushed through has already faded. Wisdom may prepare tomorrow, yet presence gives life its meaning. The past cannot be rewritten. The future cannot be entered early. Only the present ever carries weight.

Nothing more is required. Nothing less will do.

We only get one life. Do not rush through it as if another one is waiting. Goals matter. Effort matters. So does the moment you are standing in right now. Remember to enjoy the days that carry you there. Life is not something you reach. It is something you live, step by step.